if I could find God

John H. Scammon
JUDSON PRESS, VALLEY FORGE

My life makes no sense

God uses me for target practice

Yes, I've heard all that before

I give up

My hope is gone

Why won't God give me what I ask?

if I
could
find God

Anguish and Faith in the Book of Job

Everything you have said is a lie

My trouble never ends

So what if God kills me

I am angry and bitter

I am sick of living

How I wish I knew where to find him

These quotations from the Book of Job are taken from *Job for Modern Man (Today's English Version)*, Copyright, American Bible Society, 1971.

IF I COULD FIND GOD

Translations of the Bible quoted in this book are as follows:

"Job 39" from *The Bible: A New Translation* by James Moffatt. Copyright 1954 by James Moffatt. By permission of Harper & Row, Publishers, Inc.

The Holy Bible, An American Translation of the Bible. University of Chicago © 1939.

The Holy Bible, authorized King James Version (KJV).

The Holy Bible, the Revised Standard Version of the Bible (RSV), © 1946 and 1952 by the Division of Christian Education of the National Council of the Churches of Christ in the United States of America. Used by permission.

Excerpt(s) from *The Jerusalem Bible* (JB), copyright © 1966 by Darton, Longman & Todd, Ltd. and Doubleday and Company, Inc. Used by permission of the publisher.

The Living Bible (TLB). Copyright 1971 by Tyndale House Publishers, Wheaton, Illinois. Used by permission.

The Modern Language Bible (Berkeley Version). Copyright 1945, 1959, © 1969 Zondervan Publishing House. Used by permission.

Excerpts from the *New American Bible* © 1970 used herein by permission of the Confraternity of Christian Doctrine, copyright owner.

From *The New English Bible* (NEB). © The Delegates of the Oxford University Press and The Syndics of the Cambridge University Press 1961, 1970. Reprinted by permission.

Job for Modern Man, Today's English Version (TEV). Copyright, American Bible Society, 1971.

Pictures on pages 31, 45, 53, 54 taken from Robert Hodgell, illustrator, *Today's English Version of the New Testament.* Copyright © American Bible Society, 1966.

Picture on page 31 taken from Guy Rowe, illustrator, *In Our Image, Character Studies from the Old Testament,* Houston Harte, ed. (New York: Oxford University Press, 1949). Used by permission of Edward H. Harte and Houston H. Harte.

Library of Congress Cataloging in Publication Data

Scammon, John H.
If I could find God.

    (A "Do-it-yourself" Bible study book)
    Bibliography: p.
    1. Bible. O. T. Job —Study—Text-books.
I. Title.
BS1415.5.S3   223'.1'077   74-2894
ISBN 0-8170-0625-7

TO JIM AND RUTH

"I read this book as it were with my heart. . . .
You surely have read Job? Read him, read him
over and over again . . . because everything
about him is so human."

—Søren Kierkegaard[1]

[1] Søren Kierkegaard, *Repetition: An Essay in Experimental Psychology*, trans. Walter Lowrie (Princeton, N.J.: Princeton University Press, 1941), pp. 121-122. Reprinted by permission of Princeton University Press.

Acknowledgments

I wish to thank my pastor, Dr. Gene E. Bartlett, for taking time out of his busy schedule to write such a complimentary foreword. My appreciation goes also to the Messrs. Houston and Edward Harte, newspaper publishers in San Antonio and Corpus Christi, Texas, respectively, for facilitating the use of the Guy Rowe painting which was one of many exciting illustrations in their father's book, *In Our Image*. Then I am indebted to Mr. Warner A. Hutchinson, general secretary of the American Bible Society, not only for permission to reprint several sizable selections of the *Today's English Version* text of Job, but also for help in reproducing the line drawings in that text done by Mr. Robert Hodgell of the fine arts department of Eckerd College, St. Petersburg, Florida.

The National Gallery of Art, Washington, D.C., not only granted permission to use the William Blake drawing, but also assisted most helpfully in providing the copy. Thanks go to the various publishers who allowed printing of the different modern translations. I also want to thank Mr. Raymond Agler of the Boston Public Library for his help in locating the quotation from Williams' *War in Heaven*.

But the publisher of this present book, Judson Press, deserves the most appreciation, especially Frank Hoadley, acting executive director of the Division of Publishing and Business of the Board of Educational Ministries, a valued friend of many years' standing, and most of all Harold L. Twiss, managing editor of Judson Press. Nor could I forget the exceedingly painstaking help of Mrs. Phyllis A. Frantz, editorial assistant of Judson Press.

And finally my wife deserves deepest thanks for carrying so much of the burden when we were selling the house and moving into retirement—while I was trying my best to meet writing deadlines.

Foreword

If anyone needs to have confirmation that the Bible pulsates with life, he will find it in this book by John Scammon.

Professor Scammon has brought to these pages that rare combination of thorough scholarship and down-to-earth teaching for which he is noted. Humor, imagery, and contemporary allusions are all put to use in making clear the timeless and moving message of Job.

Undoubtedly many who read this book will feel that they have understood Job for the first time. They will find in it that word which illumines life, particularly the problem of suffering.

All of us who know John Scammon are grateful that he has made Job available to us with all the skill of a man born to teach and all the love of the Bible which has marked his years.

Gene E. Bartlett
Former President
American Baptist Churches
in the U.S.A.

Minister
First Baptist Church
Newton Centre, Massachusetts

Contents

A Note to the Reader   10

1. Look Where We Find Job!   11
2. Ten Ways NOT to Read the Book of Job   13
3. A Possible Outline (Until You Get a Better One)   15
4. Start Right in Reading!—But How?   19
5. What a Chapter—Job 3!   29
6. How to Get at Eliphaz's Ideas   41
7. Bildad Has Some Advice (Rusty, too)   45
8. How to Take Zophar   49
9. Now, Job!   53
10. What About Chapter 28?   61
11. The Shattered Victim's Final Defense!   65
12. Give Youth a Say!   71
13. God Himself Speaks   79
14. What Job Said Then   95
15. Is the End of the Book the Solution?   97
Postscript: The Hardest Things
   About the Book of Job: A Few Suggestions   105
Appendix: Brief Explanation of 25 Hard Terms   107
A Twelve-Inch Shelf of the Most Helpful Books   109

A Note to the Reader

The books on Job are endless, but a lay person is sometimes just swamped by the depth of some of the discussions. If this little book should serve to guide the average reader so that he or she really moves where Job moved, and hears anguished cries, then there is the possibility that a better understanding of life and of God will result. So we are not here dealing with critical questions of date and authorship. Commentaries do that. And if the present book makes great use of newer translations, it is because they have helped the writer of these lines more than he can say.

1. Look Where We Find Job!

2. Ten Ways NOT to Read the Book of Job.

1. Read only one chapter at a time, even if this does cut a speech right in half.

2. Try to find out a lot about the book before you start reading it; for example, when it was written, what the main problem is, who wrote it, etc.

3. Read poetry and prose in exactly the same way, treating each as if it made no difference. (Does it?)

4. Stick to only one translation. (But really, do you have to like a translation to profit by it?)

5. Bring to your reading some comments about Job which you have heard in the past, no matter whether the statement was based on sound knowledge or not.

6. Feel that after reading the text you can answer any questions without further helps.

7. Don't change your mind once you have made it up. Be unchangeable.

8. Assume that any statement in the book, no matter who the speaker may be, is doctrinally orthodox.

9. Assume that the powerful drama entitled *J. B.* is a retelling of the biblical book.

A N D

10. Feel that it won't be long before you have mastered the Book of Job.

THIS IS *NOT* THE WAY TO BEGIN YOUR READING OF JOB!!!!!! Now move right into the next chapter.

3. A Possible Outline
(Until You Get a Better One)

1. Opening Scene (on earth) How happy and well off can a family be!! 1:1-5	2. Second Scene (in heaven) That desperate bargain at the heavenly court! 1:6-12	3. Third Scene (back on earth) How much can a man take? 1:13-22
4. Fourth Scene (in heaven again) The celestial bargain is upped. 2:1-7a	5. Fifth Scene (back on earth) Now look at the ex-millionaire. 2:7b-10	6. Sixth Scene (still on earth) Old friends arrive on the tragic scene. 2:11-12
7. The Speeches Start (and what speeches!) Job, in unbearable agony, curses the day he was born. Chapter 3	8. Now, Three Rounds of Straight-from-the-Shoulder Outbursts (they start mildly but soon become fierce) **Eliphaz,** the first friend, opens up by gently reminding Job that all men sin, and that God corrects them. Chapters 4, 5	9. **Job** shouts that he wants to die, and asks God to let him alone. Chapters 6, 7

10. **Bildad,** the second friend, is thoroughly shocked and says bluntly that the godless are rooted out. Chapter 8	11. **Job** fights back: God destroys the innocent right along with the wicked; and why is God stalking him as if he were a hunted beast? Chapters 9, 10	12. **Zophar,** friend number three, cuts Job to the quick with the cruel word that God is punishing him less than he deserves! And Job had better come clean with God about his sin. Chapter 11
13. **Job** closes the first round of talk with the sarcastic retort that he knows as much as his friends do! But why can't God let a mere man live in peace? Chapters 12-14	14. The Second Round Starts **Eliphaz** paints a lurid picture of what happens to a man who shakes his fist at God. Chapter 15	15. **Job,** feeling that death is near, reiterates that he is an innocent man, and once more he appeals directly to God; his only hope now, however, seems to be the grave. Chapters 16, 17
16. **Bildad** mercilessly draws a horrible scene of what happens to bad people. Chapter 18	17. **Job** feels totally alienated from everybody. But after the most pitiful words in the book, in a split-second flash of confidence, he glimpses someone, someday, who will come to his defense! Chapter 19	18. **Zophar,** greatly upset, goes on where Bildad left off with how the wicked "get it," and then some! Chapter 20
19. **Job** points out that some scoundrels live very, very prosperous lives! "Everything," he winds up, "which you have said is a lie!" Chapter 21	20. The Third Round Starts **Eliphaz** tries to name Job's "sins"! What Job needs is a genuine conversion! Chapter 22	21. "How I wish I knew where to find Him," cries **Job.** "I'd present all my arguments! But I'm afraid of him!" He wonders if God is **really** just. 23; 24:1-17
22. **Bildad:** But who can really know how truly great God is? 25; 26:5-14 (In the text as we have it verses 5-14 seem to be part of Job's speech, but are really arguments that go on where chapter 25 leaves off; many credit these words to Bildad.)	23. **Job's** crisp comeback is brief and stinging. 26: 1-14	24. **Zophar** reiterates that bad people have the most awful things happen to them. 24:18-25; 27:13-23 (Again, in our text these verses seem to be spoken by Job; but they fit the opposition so much better!)

25. A remarkable poem in praise of wisdom; who is the speaker? Chapter 28	26. **Job** makes a powerful statement in his own defense. Chapters 29-31	27. Let Youth Be Heard! Angry young **Elihu** appears and talks for quite a long time! Chapters 32-37
28. The Climax: GOD HIMSELF! And He has a word to say! What questions He asks! 38:1-40:2	29. **Job's** very brief and very humble reply. 40:3-5	30. But **God** goes right on with more questions. 40:6-41:34
31. **Job's** last and best answer. 42:1-6	32. The close of the story. 42:7-17	

"**4000 years ago, a man wrote on a clay tablet in a land called Sumer, 'For me the day is black. . . . Tears, lament, anguish, and depression are lodged within me, suffering overwhelms me. . . .'"**

—S. N. Kramer [1]

[1] S. N. Kramer, "The World of Abraham," in *Everyday Life in Bible Times* (Washington, D.C.: The National Geographic Society, 1967), p. 39.

4. Start Right in Reading!
—But How?

There is no sense in wasting time; you are now ready to read Job. But it makes a *tremendous* difference how you start! Just a suggestion: try either of the following columns; perhaps you'd like to read chapter 1 in one version and chapter 2 in the other.

TODAY'S ENGLISH VERSION

Satan Tests Job

1 There was a man named Job, who lived in the land of Uz.ᵃ He worshiped God and was faithful to him. He was a good man, careful not to do anything evil. ²He had seven sons and three daughters, ³and owned 7,000 sheep, 3,000 camels, 1,000 head of cattle, and 500 donkeys. He also had a large number of servants and was by far the richest man in the East.

⁴His sons used to take turns giving a feast, to which all the others would come, and they always invited their three sisters to join them. ⁵After each feast was over, Job would get up early the next morning and offer sacrifices in

THE LIVING BIBLE

There lived in the land of Uz a man named Job—a goodᵃ man who feared God and stayed away from evil. ², ³He had a large family of seven sons and three daughters, and was immensely wealthy,ᵇ' for he owned 7,000 sheep, 3,000 camels, 500 teams of oxen, 500 female donkeys, and employed many servants. He was, in fact, the richest cattleman in that entire area.

⁴Every year when each of Job's sons had a birthday, he invited his brothers and sisters to his home for a celebration. On these occasions they would eat and drink with great merriment. ⁵When these birthday parties ended—and sometimes they lasted several days— Job would summon his children to him

order to purify his children. He always did this because he thought that one of them might have sinned by insulting God unintentionally.

⁶When the day came for the heavenly beingsᵇ to appear before the Lord, Satanᶜ was there among them. ⁷The Lord asked him, "What have you been doing?"

Satan answered, "I have been walking here and there, roaming around the earth."

⁸The Lord said, "Did you notice my servant Job? There is no one on earth as faithful and good as he is. He worships me and is careful not to do anything evil."

⁹Satan replied, "Would Job worship you if he got nothing out of it? ¹⁰You have protected him and his family and everything he owns. You bless everything he does, and you have given him enough cattle to fill the whole country. ¹¹But now suppose you take away everything he has—he will curse you to your face."

¹²The Lord said to Satan, "All right, everything he has is in your power, but you must not hurt Job himself." So Satan left.

Job's Children and Wealth Are Destroyed

¹³One day when Job's children were having a feast at the home of their oldest brother, ¹⁴a messenger came running to Job. "We were plowing the fields with the cattle," he said, "and the donkeys were in a nearby pasture. ¹⁵Suddenly the Sabeansᵈ attacked and stole them all. They killed every one of your servants except me. I am the only

---

and sanctify them, getting up early in the morning and offering a burnt offering for each of them. For Job said, "Perhaps my sons have sinned and turned away from God in their hearts." This was Job's regular practice.

⁶One day as the angelsᵈ came to present themselves before the Lord, Satan, the Accuser, came with them.

⁷"Where have you come from?" the Lord asked Satan.

And Satan replied, "From patroling the earth."

⁸Then the Lord asked Satan, "Have you noticed my servant Job? He is the finest man in all the earth—a goodᵇ man who fears God and will have nothing to do with evil."

⁹"Why shouldn't he, when you pay him so well?" Satan scoffed. ¹⁰"You have always protected him and his home and his property from all harm. You have prospered everything he does—look how rich he is! No wonder he 'worships' you! ¹¹But just take away his wealth, and you'll see him curse you to your face!"

¹², ¹³And the Lord replied to Satan, "You may do anything you like with his wealth, but don't harm him physically."

So Satan went away; and sure enough,ᵇ not long afterwards when Job's sons and daughters were dining at the oldest brother's house, tragedy struck.

¹⁴, ¹⁵A messenger rushed to Job's home with this news: "Your oxen were plowing, with the donkeys feeding beside them, when the Sabeans raided us, drove away the animals and killed all the farmhands except me. I am the only one left."

¹⁶While this messenger was still speaking, another arrived with more bad news: "The fire of God has fallen from heaven and burned up your sheep

---

ᵃ UZ: An area whose exact location is unknown.
ᵇ HEAVENLY BEINGS: Supernatural beings who serve God in heaven. ᶜ SATAN: A supernatural being whose name indicates he was regarded as man's opponent.

one who escaped to tell you."

¹⁶Before he finished speaking, another servant came and said, "Lightning struck the sheep and the shepherds and killed them all. I am the only one who escaped to tell you."

¹⁷Before he finished speaking, another servant came and said, "Three bands of Chaldean ᶜ raiders attacked us, took away the camels, and killed all your servants except me. I am the only one who escaped to tell you."

¹⁸Before he finished speaking, another servant came and said, "Your children were having a feast at the home of your oldest son, ¹⁹when a storm swept in from the desert. It blew the house down and killed them all. I am the only one who escaped to tell you."

²⁰Then Job got up and tore his clothes in grief. He shaved his head and threw himself face downward on the ground. ²¹He said, "I was born with nothing and I will die with nothing. The Lord gave, and now he has taken away. May his name be praised!" ²²In spite of everything that had happened, Job did not sin by blaming God.

Satan Tests Job Again

2 When the day came for the heavenly beings to appear before the Lord again, Satan was there among them. ²The Lord asked him, "Where have you been?"

Satan answered, "I have been walking here and there, roaming around the earth."

³The Lord asked, "Did you notice my servant Job? There is no one on earth as faithful and good as he is. He worships me and is careful not to do anything evil. You persuaded me to let

---

and all the herdsmen, and I alone have escaped to tell you."

¹⁷Before this man finished, still another messenger rushed in: "Three bands of Chaldeans have driven off your camels and killed your servants, and I alone have escaped to tell you."

¹⁸As he was still speaking, another arrived to say, "Your sons and daughters were feasting in their oldest brother's home, ¹⁹When suddenly a mighty wind swept in from the desert, and engulfed the house so that the roof fell in on them and all are dead; and I alone escaped to tell you."

²⁰Then Job stood up and tore his robe in grief ᵉ and fell down upon the ground before God. ²¹"I came naked from my mother's womb," he said, "And I shall have nothing when I die. The Lord gave me everything I had, and they were His to take away. Blessed be the name of the Lord."

²²In all of this, Job did not sin or revile God.

CHAPTER 2

N ow the angels ᵃ came again to present themselves before the Lord, and Satan with them.

²"Where have you come from?" the Lord asked Satan.

"From patroling the earth," Satan replied.

³"Well, have you noticed My servant Job?" the Lord asked. "He is the finest man in all the earth—a good man who fears God and turns away from all evil. And he has kept his faith in Me despite the fact that you persuaded Me to let you harm him without any cause."

a Literally, "upright."
b Implied.
c Literally, "have cursed God."
d Literally, "the sons of God."
e Literally, "tore his robe and shaved his head."

---

d SABEANS: A tribe of wandering raiders from the south. ᵉ CHALDEANS: A tribe of wandering raiders from the north.

you attack him for no reason at all, but Job is still as faithful as ever."

⁴Satan replied, "A man will give up everything in order to stay alive. ⁵But now suppose you hurt his body—he will curse you to your face."

⁶So the Lord said to Satan, "All right, he is in your power, but you are not to kill him."

⁷Then Satan left the Lord's presence and made sores break out all over Job's body. ⁸Job went and sat by the garbage dump and took a piece of broken pottery to scrape his sores. ⁹His wife said to him, "You are still as faithful as ever, aren't you? Why don't you curse God and die?"

¹⁰Job answered, "You are talking nonsense! When God sends us something good we welcome it. How can we complain when he sends us trouble?" Even in all this suffering Job did not say anything against God.

Job's Friends Come

¹¹Three of Job's friends were Eliphaz, from the city of Teman,ᶠ Bildad, from the land of Shuah,ᵍ and Zophar, from the land of Namah.ʰ When they heard how much Job had been suffering, they decided to go visit him and comfort him. ¹²While they were still a long way off they saw Job, but did not recognize him. When they did, they began to weep and wail. They tore their clothes in grief and threw dust into the air and on their heads. ¹³Then they sat there on the ground with him for seven days and nights without saying a word, because they saw how much he was suffering.

ᶠ TEMAN: A city in the country of Edom, southeast of Palestine. ᵍSHUAH: A region possibly near the Euphrates River, or perhaps in northern Arabia. ʰ NAMAH: A region whose exact location is unknown.

⁴˒⁵"Skin for skin," Satan replied, "A man will give anything to save his life. Touch his body with sickness and he will curse You to Your face!"

⁶"Do with him as you please," the Lord replied; "only spare his life."

⁷So Satan went out from the presence of the Lord and struck Job with a terrible case of boils from head to foot. ⁸Then Job took a broken piece of pottery to scrape himself, and sat among the ashes.

⁹His wife said to him, "Are you still trying to be godly when God has done all this to you? Curse Him and die."

¹⁰But he replied, "You talk like some heathen woman. What? Shall we receive only pleasant things from the hand of God and never anything unpleasant?" So in all this Job said nothing wrong.

¹¹When three of Job's friends heard of all the tragedy that had befallen him, they got in touch with each other and traveled from their homes to comfort and console him. Their names were Eliphaz the Temanite, Bildad the Shuhite, and Zophar the Naamathite. ¹²Job was so changed that they could scarcely recognize him. Wailing loudly in despair, they tore their robes and threw dust into the air and put earth on their heads to demonstrate their sorrow. ¹³Then they sat upon the ground with him silently for seven days and nights, no one speaking a word; for they saw that his suffering was too great for words.

ᵃ Literally, "sons of God."

WHERE WAS UZ?

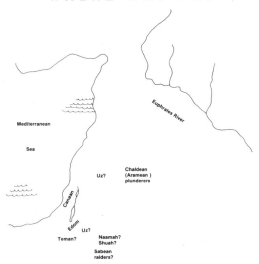

But Uz is any place in the world where good people suffer beyond what they deserve!

You can't really read the Bible unless you see the people, watch them move about, and hear the sound of their voices. Can you begin to see the principal figures in these two startling chapters? Here they are;

Job, a very, very, very rich property owner of Uz, a man of irreproachable character and authentic religion.

His wife, their seven grown-up sons, and three fine daughters.

The three longtime friends, probably natives of Edom:

Eliphaz, of Teman in Edom; an older man, kindly by nature, deeply religious, even mystical.

Bildad, of Shuah (location unknown); less sympathetic, a hidebound traditionalist ("it was good enough for grampa, it's good enough for me" type).

Zophar, of Naamah (again, location unknown); a rough, coarse-grained, browbeating dogmatist.

Elihu, an "angry young man," very cocky with all the answers.

The Satan or Accuser, a sort of prosecuting attorney of the heavenly court. In the Hebrew text the article is always used—the Satan. (See the Appendix: Brief Explanation of 25 Hard Terms.)

God himself, creator of the universe, ruler of all things, and head of the heavenly court.

Sons of God, the heavenly court, made up of superhuman beings, carrying out God's directives.

Now tell the story contained in these two chapters in your own words, aloud if possible, starting somewhat as follows, and making it just as vivid as you possibly can:

Scene One. On earth. Job ....

Scene Two. In heaven. God ....

Scene Three. Back on earth. As Job ....

Scene Four. In heaven again. The heavenly court is in session again, and ....

Scene Five. Now look at Job, the ex-millionaire ....

SOME MORE THINGS TO THINK ABOUT
IF AND WHEN YOU HAVE TIME

One hundred and one questions come to mind when one really begins to read between the lines of these two harrowing chapters. One adult class raised the following:

1. Why was the Satan allowed to do this job? Why did God let Satan talk him into tormenting Job to see if Job would curse God, especially since God was convinced Job wouldn't?

2. Job was so upright; but why does it say that he merely avoided sinning without mentioning any positive acts of good?

3. If God wanted to hurt Job, why did he not take his wife away and thereby make him completely alone?

4. Why didn't the other heavenly beings try to dissuade the Satan from harming Job?

5. Why did God create the Satan? Why was he among the heavenly beings?

6. Were Job's children godly?

7. In what capacity did the Satan patrol the earth?

8. Can a God who would use Job as a testing ground in a debate really be a God whom we can trust?

9. Why would God ask the Satan where he had been? Wouldn't he know?

10. Why did Job have any faith left after what had happened?

11. How could Job endure so much?

Perhaps you want to add some questions of your own:

NOW LET'S READ A LITTLE MORE BETWEEN THE LINES

Imagine how the news about Job's awful tragedies reached the three friends; how they got in touch with one another; the trip to Uz; what the conversation was like on the way; the sight that finally met their eyes (2:12).

Now ask, does it make any difference that the time of these events seems that of the patriarchal age? Do the same things happen (though not in exact detail) in every generation? In an urban as well as in an agrarian society?

Can you now raise various possibilities as to what the purpose of the writing of the book was?

Was it to ask: how much can a man take and keep his faith?

Or: will a man be religious unless God rewards him in some way?

Or: granted that God is all-powerful, is he just?

Or: how can a good God allow good people to suffer so much?

Or: is God really a friend of Job, or an enemy?

Let's raise the question, could you or I lose practically everything and say what Job said in 1:21?

Let's think more, too, about Job's wife. One tradition has her cutting off and selling her hair in order to support Job in his poverty. But the Septuagint version (translation of the Old Testament from Hebrew to Greek, completed by the time of Jesus Christ) of Job 2:9 may be translated:

And when much time had passed, his wife said to him, How long wilt thou hold out, saying, Behold, I wait yet a little while, expecting the hope of my deliverance? for, behold, thy memorial is abolished from the earth, *even thy* sons and daughters, the pangs and pains of my womb which I bore in vain with sorrows; and thou thyself sittest down to spend the nights in the open air among the corruption of worms, and I am a wanderer and a servant from place to place and house to house, waiting for the setting of the sun, that I may rest from my labours and my pangs which now beset me: but say some word against the Lord, and die. [2]

There are some very interesting rabbinical stories built around Job's wife. Let's quote just one:

While the three kings (comforters) were conversing thus with Job, his wife . . . made her appearance clad in rags, and she threw herself at the feet of her husband's friends, and amid tears . . . "O Eliphaz, and ye other friends of Job, remember what I was in other days, and how I am now changed, coming before you in rags and tatters." The sight of the unhappy woman touched them so deeply that they could only weep, and not a word could they force out of their mouths. Eliphaz, however, took his royal mantle of purple, and laid it about the shoulders of the poor woman. (Job's wife) asked only one favor, that the three kings should order their soldiers to clear away the ruins of the building under which her children lay entombed, that she might give their remains decent burial. The command was issued to the soldiers accordingly, but Job said, "Do not put yourselves to trouble for naught. My children will not be found, for they are safely bestowed with their Lord and Creator." Again his friends were sure that Job was bereft of his senses. He arose, however, prayed to God, and at the end of his devotions, he bade his friends look eastward, and when they did his bidding, they beheld his children next to the Ruler of heaven, with crowns of glory on their heads. (Job's wife) prostrated herself, and said, "Now I know that my memorial resides with the Lord." [3]

Now you probably want to ask, what was Job's disease? You won't get very far trying to diagnose it; there have been many, many theories. It has been called elephantiasis, a thickening and cracking of the skin, plus enormous enlarging of the affected parts; leprosy (this would account for his banishment outside the village); Baghdad Button or Jericho Rose, characterized by ulcerous boils; *pemphigus*

[2] Job 2:9, *The Septuagint Version of the Old Testament* (London: S. Bagster and Sons Limited, n.d.).
[3] Louis Ginzberg, *The Legends of the Jews* (Philadelphia: Jewish Publication Society of America, 1910), vol. 2, pp. 238-239.

foliaceus, with bulbous inflammation which comes on very rapidly and develops into blistering, with offensive odors, emaciation, cycles of improvement and then relapse, and finally death. If you wish to look ahead in the book to references to Job's condition, see 7:5, 14; 16:8, 16; 17:7, 14; 19:17, 20; 21:5; 30:17, 27, 30. We do not know just what the disease was, but Job was sure he was dying (10:20, 21; 17:1). Be sure to look up these passages!

Where was Job in 2:8? The Septuagint says "on a dunghill." Terrien is very vivid: " . . . Job left his house for a heap of dung ashes—the *mazbala,* which exists to this day outside Arabian towns—and there he sat, amid rubbish, rotting carcasses, playing urchins, homeless beggars, village idiots, and howling dogs. The respected prince was now an outcast, awaiting death, tormented by pain, and rent by mental anguish." [4]

Notice that *Today's English Version* translates it not "ashes" or "dunghill" but "garbage dump." It certainly wasn't a pleasant spot. Dry animal dung (plus other things, no doubt) was brought day after day, month after month, and year after year from the village, was burned perhaps once a month, and was packed down by rains until an extensive hill of dung ashes stood there. It became high enough and large enough to serve, sometimes, as a watchtower. Except for remaining smells and unsavory attendants, it made a good place, because of its height, to catch the evening breeze.

Verse 4 in chapter 2 is very difficult. Is it a popular saying of which we do not know the exact significance? If you read different commentaries, you may find that each has a different interpretation.

Finally, notice that Job's friends first of all sat down with him in that stinking hole. Isn't it true that when friends lose their dearest, they will soon forget what we said to them, but will remember that we came?

---

[4] Samuel Terrien, "The Book of Job, Introduction and Exegesis," *The Interpreter's Bible,* ed. George A. Buttrick, et al. (Nashville: Abingdon Press, 1954), vol. 3, p. 920.

The Modern Language Bible makes reference to Job's "fist of defiance." This is a good description.

---

5. What a Chapter—Job 3!

Try to do three things as you start to read Job 3.

First, get into the mood just as much as you possibly can. Perhaps this question, once asked of a pioneer radio preacher, S. Parkes Cadman, will help:

> I am a man 74 years of age, and I find myself utterly unable to explain the following situations. In 1895 my wife, sick with melancholia, took her own life. In 1901 my eldest son died of a fever. In 1920 my eldest daughter committed suicide during a period of mental depression. In 1924 my only remaining son and his two children were burned to death in their own home. My questions about life can be summed up in one word, "Why?"

Second, stop long enough to think what a person says today when life suddenly caves in for him and he loses practically everything. Here are a few possibilities:

"Why *me?* What have *I* done?"

"Where was God when my family was wiped out?"

"A good God would never let this happen to a person who has always tried to do right as I have!"

What do you think you would have said?

(Write the answer down in this space.)

Third, try to picture what is going on as if it were taking place right in front of your eyes. Here are three pictures, the first by the well-known English poet and artist William Blake (1757–1827), the second by Robert Hodgell, the illustrator of *Job for Modern Man (Today's English Version),* and the third by Guy Rowe, a great character portraitist who once did *Time* magazine covers.

Which, if any, of these pictures does justice to the scene?

William Blake, National Gallery of Art, Washington, D.C., Rosenwald Collection.

"The Book of Job," pl. 7,   "And when they lifted up their eyes afar off and knew him not, they lifted up their voice and wept."

Let's read now the vivid translation of Job's cry of pain in the *Jerusalem Bible;* some comments will be suggested, but you will add the best ones. Please write down after each set of sentences whatever comes to your mind (questions, reactions, insights). This will take some of your time but is worth every minute you spend on it. Try it out and see!

Incidentally, if you like outlines, the chapter may be divided into Job's curse (vv. 3-10); Job's question (11-19); and Job's cry (20-26). And one more word: if you are surprised that a sufferer (who is sure that he is dying) can speak in such magnificent poetry, don't let the superb literary quality of this masterpiece make the agony of the central character seem any less real.

Now try to hear Job's anguished voice as it rises and falls.

In the end it was Job who broke the silence and cursed the day of his birth. This is what he said: (3:1,2.)

Comments

Why hadn't the three friends tried to say something helpful long before this? Had they waited for Job to speak because he was the oldest one there (or wasn't he?—see 15:10)? Some writers say that customarily the bereaved person spoke first. Kenneth Taylor's rendering in his *Living Lessons of Life and Love* is: "Let the day of my birth be damned!"

Did *you* ever wish you'd never been born?

"May the day perish when I was born,
and the night that told of a boy conceived.
May that day be darkness,
may God on high have no thought for it,
may no light shine on it.
May murk and deep shadow claim it for their own,
clouds hang over it,
eclipse swoop down on it.
Yes, let the dark lay hold of it,
to the days of the year let it not be joined,
into the reckoning of months not find its way.
May that night be dismal,
no shout of joy come near it." (3:3-7)

Comments

Phrase after phrase expresses the idea of deep, impenetrable darkness. What is the blackest, most "scary" place you've ever been in?

The implication here is something like this: "I'd like to take a calendar for the year in which I was born; and with a soft, black crayon completely smudge out my birthday!"

"Let them curse it who curse the day,
   who are prepared to rouse Leviathan." (3:8)

Or here is *Today's English Version:*
   "Tell the sorcerers to curse that day, those who know how to command Leviathan,"

Then follows a footnote: "Sorcerers: Magicians who claimed to be able to do such things as make a day unlucky. Leviathan: An imaginary monster, sometimes identified with the crocodile. Magicians were thought to be able to make him do such work as causing eclipses of the sun."

Comments

"Dark be the stars of its morning,
   let it wait in vain for light
   and never see the opening eyes of dawn.
Since it would not shut the doors of the womb on me
   to hide sorrow from my eyes." (3:9,10)

Comments

Which of the following statements seems to you closest to the truth? In this chapter, Job, following the awful blows which have struck him down, seems—

frenzied
numb from shock
bitter
at his wit's end
tormented more by mental and spiritual pain than
by physical agony

"Why did I not die newborn,
not perish as I left the womb?
Why were there two knees to receive me,
two breasts for me to suck?
Had there not been, I should now be lying in peace." (3:11-13)

Comments

Did you ever wish you had been born dead?

"wrapped in a restful slumber,
with the kings and high viziers of earth
who built themselves vast vaults," (3:14)

Comments

Some think the reference is to the building of the gigantic pyramids
of Egypt; others take it as a general reference to the restoration of
ancient ruins.

"or with princes who have gold and to spare
and houses crammed with silver." (3:15)

Comments

Ever wonder how it would feel to be in this situation?

"Or put away like a stillborn child that never came to be,
like unborn babies that never see the light." (3:16)

Comments

Stillborn babies—we've all seen the tragic disappointment of parents
after months of preparation and waiting. Job in his anguish wishes he
had been born without any life in him!

"Down there, bad men bustle no more,
there the weary rest." (3:17)

This is so much more beautiful in the King James translation. (The
King James Version is the most beautiful we shall ever read, but not
the most understandable, because of changes in languages and of new
manuscript discoveries; see verses 8b, 12a, for example.) The *King*

James Version reads like pure rhythmic poetry:

Thére the wícked ceáse from troúbling;
And thére the wéary bé at rést.   (Accents added)

Comments

"Prisoners, all left in peace,
   hear no more the shouts of the jailer.
Down there, high and low are all one,
   and the slave is free of his master." (3:18, 19)

Comments

Death is the great leveler!

"Why give light to a man of grief?
   Why give life to those bitter of heart." (3:20)

Comments

"Who long for a death that never comes,
and hunt for it more than for a buried treasure?
They would be glad to see the grave mound
and shout with joy if they reached the tomb." (3:21, 22)

Comments

Think of some reasons why certain people want to die more than anything else.

"Why make this gift of light to a man who does not see his way,
whom God balks on every side?" (3:23)

Comments

For the first time, Job now makes reference to God! But it is to a God who seems to him to be completely hostile.

"My only food is sighs,
and my groans pour out like water." (3:24)

Comments

Stop a moment and give a heavy sigh; then, a genuine groan. Exactly how does this make you feel?

"Whatever I fear comes true,
    Whatever I dread befalls me.
For me, there is no calm, no peace;
    my torments banish rest." (3:25, 26)

Moffatt's translation: "I get no peace, I get no rest, I get no ease. ...."

Comments

How many people there are in the world who feel this way this very minute!

You might like to look up, in books on the subject, what were the terrifying fears of famous people of the past! Isaac Newton, for example; de Maupassant, etc. Numerous books have been written on the subject of fear.

SOME MORE THINGS TO THINK ABOUT

This chapter reminds me of what an older friend wrote back when I tried to console him over the loss of his beloved wife. "It's all right, John, until it happens to *you*. Then it's different."

You surely sense that Job's mood in this chapter is not at all that of 1:21 and 2:10. Do not be in a hurry to account for the radical change. We shall come back to this.

Compare Job 3 with Jeremiah 20:14-18.

Why do you suppose that Job seems to ignore, entirely, his three friends who came to comfort him?

Do you think a person should read this speech several times? How many? In more than one translation? Why?

"The friends are like men who close their eyes to the real facts, rock back on their heels, and speak of general principles, every one of which is being called into serious question by the indisputable facts before them."

—Balmer H. Kelly[1]

[1] Balmer H. Kelly, "The Book of Job," *The Layman's Bible Commentary*, vol. 8 (Richmond: John Knox Press, 1962), p. 67.

6. How to Get at Eliphaz's Ideas

The procedure in the next four chapters will be as follows: Instead of reading the chapters of Job between 4 and 27 in the biblical order, we'll first take the three speeches of the older man, Eliphaz, all together, and really get acquainted with him as he becomes less and less friendly and more and more bluntly accusing. Then the same will be done for the hidebound traditionalist, Bildad; and dogmatic Zophar will occupy chapter 8 of our study as he throws his weight around. This procedure can be justified because actually the speakers do not consistently (sometimes not at all) reply to one another so much as air their own theological beliefs.

This time take your favorite translation of the Bible and read (at one sitting, if possible, and without stopping to write any comments) the following chapters: 4, 5, 15, 22. Here is a quick summary of what Eliphaz says:

Job has helped others;
   how come he can't take it himself?
Job knows, as Eliphaz knows—
   good people aren't punished;
   only bad people get it.
Eliphaz once had a somewhat terrifying religious experience:

he learned that everybody is unworthy and impure before
God.
Job ought to know—
Bad people have troubles galore!
Why doesn't Job try God?
Talk directly to him, Job!
God really cares for those who are in trouble!
How happy—
is the person whom God corrects. [2]
Job—turn to him—
and everything will be fine again.
Job's words are just so much hot air!
He is shockingly irreverent!
Furthermore, Job's conscience is hurting—
but he doesn't let on.
Job doesn't know as much
as he thinks he does!
Everybody is corrupt—
that's all there is to it.
Remember what we learn from the past:
No man who shakes his fist at God will get away with it!
The wicked get punished and then some.
God stands in no need of man's goodness;
he gets no benefit from human piety.
Job is taking it on the chin because of all the evil he's done
to the poor, the hungry, to widows, to orphans.
Job, remember—
God sees!
If Job will only yield, make peace with God,
throw his gold away, make God his treasure,
then he'll enjoy God and succeed in everything he does!

Now are you ready to tackle some of these questions?
How do you picture Eliphaz? As he speaks, is he sitting or moving
around?

[2] Remember this in connection with Elihu later on.

Where does he think trouble comes from? For what purpose? Why does he become less kindly as he goes along? His hair-raising religious experience is very much worth studying. Describe this to yourself. Do many have such an experience? Would you be interested in a classic study by William James, *The Varieties of Religious Experience?*
Exactly what does Eliphaz believe about God?
What is his most helpful idea? His least impressive one?
How much of his thinking do you agree with?
Do you know a modern Eliphaz?

"Bildad is devoted to the works of the fathers. He rushes to their defense, seizing upon the first quotations that come to mind; he can do little but quote."

—Margaret B. Crook [1]

"He (Bildad) is probably a nervous, impulsive, extremely convinced believer, whose religious feelings have been painfully hurt."

—Samuel Terrien [2]

---

[1] Margaret B. Crook, *The Cruel God* (Boston: Beacon Press, 1959), p. 51.
[2] Samuel Terrien, "The Book of Job, Introduction and Exegesis," *The Interpreter's Bible*, ed. George A. Buttrick, et al. (Nashville: Abingdon Press, 1954), vol. 3, p. 970.

7. Bildad Has Some Advice
(Rusty, too)

This is the way Robert Hodgell sketches Bildad's features in *Today's English Version*. What quick impression do you get? As you read this chapter, come back to this drawing and see if you think it's a reasonable likeness of the way Job's second friend may have looked.

Skip this next paragraph of suggestions if you wish and get right into the meat of Bildad's speech. (But I really hope you won't!) You see, there are different ways of trying to get the feel of the words and of hearing his voice rising and falling. One way, in study groups, is to have four readers (reasonably good ones) take the parts of Job, Eliphaz, Bildad, and Zophar. Make sure they really let go! Or *you* can take, in turn, the four parts yourself and read them aloud. But do it when you're alone and when the TV isn't competing! The least effective way is to read silently. If you do this, there are still two helpful possibilities: you can read chapters 3—27 and 29—31 in order (probably not at one time; that would be a large order!); or, as was suggested in the last chapter, you can take the three outbursts of each of the three friends lumped together (since often the speaker in this book does not answer the preceding argument).

What did Bildad say? First, turn back to the outline of the book in chapter 3 and read sections 10, 16, and 22. Then read in *Today's English Version* this time:

    chapter 8
    chapter 18
    chapter 25
    and also 26:5-14 (see the explanation in *Today's English Version* for including this last section).

In chapter 8 of the Book of Job we catch Bildad's spirit. He says two things which come to his mind as he reels over the shock of hearing Job's agonized, wild words against God. He has one tight theory that fits absolutely all cases. It is this: What you get in life exactly and absolutely matches the kind of person you are. So, to Bildad, Job's life must have had some pretty bad spots in it to match his present agony. (See 8:4, a cruel statement if there ever was one!) Do you feel as you read this speech like saying, "Rubbish!"? And Bildad adds that this is no private discovery of his, but that everybody had known it for a hundred years or more because grandfather's theology books all said so (8:8-10, somewhat modernized!). Chapter 18 draws a horrible picture of what always happens to bad people. And chapters 25 and 26:5-14 contain a striking and reverent tribute to the awful power of God in his universe.

Now, how do you react to Bildad? *Can* one judge a person's

character by his prosperity? Are the steps of bad people continually dogged by crushing misfortune?

Check the statements which most nearly tell, in your judgment, the truth about him:

He was a hidebound traditionalist.

His theology was lifeless and mechanical.

He was the kind of person who would say, "It was good enough for grampa; it's good enough for me!"

Bildad's theology never included any new ideas. It was all found in the musty old books published generations before.

But can't we say anything good about him? Yes. Bildad's last speech certainly is a noble statement of the awe-inspiring omnipotence of God. And some writers feel that in chapter 8 the hard, relentless ring of his voice changes in verses 20-22 to a somewhat softened appeal to Job to trust God's help and turn back to him.

We cannot help being hard on Bildad. But haven't *we* ever thought or spoken in the same vein? A friend's family suffers an awful tragedy. Someone says, "Well, it must have been the will of God. Only we don't understand." Here is Bildad's tight, lifeless, mechanical dogma all over again.

SOME MORE THINGS TO THINK ABOUT

Try making a list of the crooks you've known about who "got theirs," and in a hurry; then try a list of *those who didn't!*

Isn't the "old timer" needed with his advice from yesterday?

Why are we sometimes so cruel in what we say to a suffering friend!

How can one "keep up" in his religious thinking?

Bildad says that man is a "worm," but says it in the light of God's awful omnipotence and purity and power (25:6). A famous old hymn by Isaac Watts contained the words, "Would He devote that sacred head, for such a worm as I?" In what sense is man a worm, and in what sense isn't he?

What steps have you discovered for overcoming the generation gap?

H. H. Rowley calls Zophar "the coarsest" of the three friends.[1]

_____

[1]"Job," *The Century Bible* (Camden: Thomas Nelson Inc., 1970), p. 3.

8. How to Take Zophar

Are you getting a little tired of the three "friends" or "comforters" and their lengthy speeches? Zophar is the last one of the trio.

Before you read what this man had to say, try to imagine how you would have presented those three longtime acquaintances who had come a long way to see their crushed friend. Imagine what kind of words you would have put in their mouths if you had been the inspired writer. Take two minutes to think this over.

Now I suggest that you read this time in the *Revised Standard Version* the following:

chapter 11
chapter 20
chapters 24:18-25 and 27:13-23.[2]

Speech one. In a stinging rebuke Zophar cruelly says that Job is suffering less than he deserves (11:6). How in the world could one say this to a friend who is going through a shattering tragedy? Zophar wonders how Job can possibly think that he can understand God; nobody can! God is too great! Then Zophar gets really sarcastic and

[2] The Hebrew text contains no third speech by Zophar. However, these verses, which are here in the mouth of Job, really argue against what Job has been saying, and fit the ideas of Zophar "to a T." See the footnote in *Today's English Version*.

says "a stupid man will get understanding, when a wild ass's colt is born a man" (11:12, RSV)! Some of the other translations have other possible renderings.

Speech two. He goes on with the most lurid and horrible pictures of how the wicked "get it."

Speech three. More of the same.

Perhaps the best way to wind up the study of the ideas of the three friends is to look very carefully at the chart on page 51. Feel free to add to it in your own handwriting.

SOME MORE THINGS TO THINK ABOUT

Which one of the three friends could you stand best if he were under the same roof with you?

Do you know any people who have ideas much like one of them?

You may not feel that we have been fair to one of the three. Feel free to disagree!

Sir Arthur Quiller-Couch wrote, "I find Eliphaz more of a personage than the other two; grander in the volume of his mind, securer in wisdom; as I find Zophar rather noticeably a mean-minded greybeard, and Bildad a man of the stand-no-nonsense kind."[3]

[3]Sir Arthur Quiller-Couch, *On the Art of Reading* (New York: G. P. Putnam's Sons, 1920), p. 204.

	ELIPHAZ "The Mystic" Chapters 4, 5, 15, 22	BILDAD "The Traditionalist" Chapters 8, 18, 25, 26:5-14	ZOPHAR "The Dogmatist" Chapters 11, 20, 24:18-25, 27:13-23
BELIEF ABOUT JOB'S SUFFERING	First Eliphaz drops a hint that Job is hiding some secret sin (5:6); then in the third address he bluntly tells Job he has led a very callous, unfeeling life (22:5-9); that's why he's now having so many tragedies.	Job's suffering is caused by his wrongdoing—that's all there is to it!	Job's suffering is less than he deserves!
BELIEF ABOUT SUFFERING IN GENERAL	Suffering may be sent by God for disciplinary rather than punitive purposes (5:17 suggests this). But it is also the bad man's dreadful and uncompromising reward (22:16).	What you get in life exactly matches the person you are; therefore all misfortune is the result of sin (8:13, 20).	Same as what Bildad said, only more so! (20:4-29).
BELIEF ABOUT GOD	God alone is good (15:15); he is just and punishes wrongdoing in no uncertain terms (15:20 ff.). He is too far above us to be affected by what we do, and is completely impartial in his justice (22:3-5), but he accepts the man who repents, and rewards him (22:23-30).	God is absolutely omnipotent (26:5-14a); absolutely just (8:3); and absolutely transcendent (26:14b).	God's mind is unsearchable and beyond our understanding (11:7); but one thing is certain—he is inflexibly just! (20:29).
KEY VERSE	5:17	8:8, 13	11:5, 6
SUGGESTION AS TO WHAT JOB OUGHT TO DO	Commit himself and his condition to God (5:8); if he gets rid of the wrongdoing in his life, God will make things look up for him (22:23, 27a, 28b).	Get back to God! (8:5-7).	Job had better come clean with God about his sins, or else—(11:13-20).

"His (Job's) language does not stop short of blasphemy."

—Julius A. Bewer [1]

---

[1] Julius A. Bewer, *The Literature of the Old Testament* (New York: Columbia University Press, 1962), p. 335.

9. Now, Job!

You'd better be prepared for some white-hot language as you begin this section!

First, in order to get into Job's feelings, study the way Robert Hodgell imagines that Job's face changes as the arguments go on

DURING THE FIRST SPEECH: **DURING THE THIRD SPEECH:**

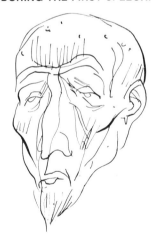 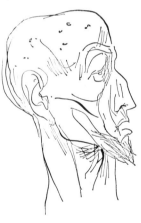

THEN, THE FOURTH:

AND THE SEVENTH:

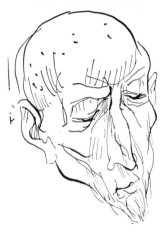

What do you read into these illustrations? Do you think they portray Job's feelings correctly?

Warning: Do not expect the arguments to be like a lawyer's brief. H. Wheeler Robinson writes: "A man suffering the torment of physical and mental pain does not think logically and progressively. His thoughts are instinctive."[2]

There is no substitute for reading the Scripture text itself, and reading from two translations is better than reading from one. Once more let it be said, you do not need to like a translation to profit from it. Now, would it be possible for you to set aside one hour in which to read these great passages without interruption?

[2] H. Wheeler Robinson, *The Cross in the Old Testament* (Philadelphia: The Westminster Press, 1955), p. 19.

chapters 6, 7   — 1st speech
chapters 9, 10   — 2nd speech
chapters 12, 13, 14   — 3rd speech
chapters 16, 17   — 4th speech
chapter 19   — 5th speech
chapter 21   — 6th speech
chapters 23, 24:1-17 — 7th speech

It is extremely helpful to write down a brief summary, in your own words, of what is being said. For example:

First Speech: *Job speaks in very bitter and outspoken language, accusing God of having shot poisoned arrows into his body. If only God would just finish him off! But he is an innocent man! Even his friends, whom he has known so long, have completely let him down. Why won't God even let him alone long enough so he can swallow his spit?*

Second Speech: *God is so great that puny man can't get anywhere with him; in fact, he destroys innocent and wicked alike! If only there might be someone to arbitrate between Job and God! At any rate, let God stop laying his rod on Job's back. Job is so sick of living!*

Third Speech: *Job retorts to his three friends that he knows as much as they do; in fact, they don't know as much in some ways as the birds and the animals do! What he wants most of all is to talk directly to God, face to face! If only God would stop hitting him and scaring him so! But God is hiding from him. If he could only die—and just possibly, God might call him back, this time as his friend.*

Will you now do the same for the rest of the speeches, writing three or four sentences for each one, in your own words, as vividly as possible?

Fourth Speech:

Fifth Speech (this is a very exciting one):

Sixth Speech:

Seventh Speech:

The second part of your study of these powerful passages centers on the explanation of three key words: Umpire (9:33), Witness (16:19), Redeemer (19:25-27).

Umpire: The King James translation here is "daysman," a now obsolete term for "arbiter." The term "umpire" has nothing to do with sports; think rather of the area of disputes, where arbitration is often so helpful. Try different translations of this verse. What Job is crying out for is a go-between! It is a bold figure of one who would lay his hand on both Job's and God's shoulders to make a decision between them.

Witness: Here again Job desperately longs for an intermediary to plead with God for him. And suddenly he becomes aware of such a one, although he does not spell out all that this involves, much as we wish he had!

Redeemer: (Be sure to look up the explanatory material in the Appendix.) On these three verses Terrien remarks, "Thus the final plea to men makes room for the most momentous expression of faith which may be found in the poem and perhaps in the entire Hebrew Bible. . . ."[3] While the text is very, very difficult (see the commentaries), Job surely gets hold of something wonderful, deep, and temporarily satisfying to him. As Terrien writes further, ". . . at this climactic moment he shouts, 'But I know that my defender lives! He will survive my unjust death, and over the dust of my grave . . . he will stand at the last instant. Through his intermediation, by his activity, he will summon God and me together, and bring me before the face of God!' . . . the passage foreshadows an obstinacy of faith which transcends the limitations of the original poem. Christian interpreters—as well as the innumerable hearers of Handel's oratorio, *The Messiah*—have a right to find in this passage a prefiguration of the Christian experience of salvation."[4]

Is a groundwork being laid here which should lead the Christian straight into the New Testament?

[3] Samuel Terrien, "The Book of Job, Introduction and Exegesis," *The Interpreter's Bible*, ed. George A. Buttrick, et al. (Nashville: Abingdon Press, 1954), vol. 3, p. 1051.
[4] *Ibid.*, pp. 1052-1053.

You Surely Have Comments

SOME MORE THINGS TO THINK ABOUT

You will certainly want to consult some other books on the greatest single passage in Job's speeches, 19:25-27. Please look right now for a moment at the section "A Twelve-Inch Shelf of the Most Helpful Books" on Job at the end of this book. The further you go in the study of these verses, the more you will be both baffled and rewarded! (How we wish Job had explained himself much more fully!) Here is a literal translation of the Hebrew text: "But as for me, I know that my redeemer lives, and at last upon dust he will stand (or, arise). And after my skin they destroy this and from my flesh I shall see God, whom I myself shall see for myself (or, for me) and my eyes shall see and not a strange one; my insides are spent (or, are at an end) inside me."

If you are reading the *King James Version,* notice the words in italics (this means that such words are not found in the Hebrew). How many translations can you find on this key passage, with the help of your public library, perhaps a church library, and with the aid of your minister? You would find some helpful renderings if you would compare several, for example: *The Living Bible,* the *New American Bible, The New English Bible, The Modern Language Bible, The Jerusalem Bible, The American Standard Bible, A New Translation* (Moffatt), the Smith-Goodspeed translation, *The Revised Standard Version,* and *Today's English Version.* All of these have been translated in the last fifty years!

Now notice the things which Job does *not* do in his agony!

He never doubts the existence of an omnipotent being. See, for example, 9:9, 10. He does not say that he is a sinless person. See 7:21; 10:15; 13:26b; 14:17. He never contemplates suicide (very rare in the Bible; how many cases can you find?). Are you beginning to understand Job *as a person*, not as a character in a book? He knows that he is a man of integrity (9:21; 23:11, 12). A helpful study entitled "Job's Personality—What Kind of Man Was Job?" is found in Richard Singer's *Job's Encounter*, a study by a man who was ordained as a Reformed Jewish rabbi and who has also done much work in the field of psychology.[5] This and the companion volume, which is edited by Raymond Breakstone, *Job: A Case Study*,[6] contain, besides teaching guides to use in a class, such writings as Archibald MacLeish's *J. B.*, Robert Frost's *A Masque of Reason*, and a valuable résumé of the book of Job, plus older and newer interpretations.

[5] Richard E. Singer, *Job's Encounter* (New York: Bookman Associates, imprint of Twayne Publishers, Inc., 1963), pp. 170-183.
[6] *Job: A Case Study*, ed. Raymond Breakstone (New York: Bookman Associates, imprint of Twayne Publishers, Inc., 1964).

"A musical interlude."

—Samuel Terrien[1]

_____

[1] Samuel Terrien, "The Book of Job, Introduction and Exegesis," *The Interpreter's Bible*, ed. George A. Buttrick, et al. (Nashville: Abingdon Press, 1954), vol. 3, p. 1100.

10. What About Chapter 28?

Chapter 28 comes as a real surprise. It is a *magnificent* poem about wisdom. After you read it, you may say, "This is marvelous, but what is it doing here?"

That's what most writers on the chapter say. But read it yourself several times and in several translations. Here it is in the *New English Bible:*

GOD'S UNFATHOMABLE WISDOM

There are mines for silver
and places where men refine gold;
where iron is won from the earth
and copper smelted from the ore;
the end of the seam lies in darkness,
and it is followed to its farthest limit.
Strangers cut the galleries;
they are forgotten as they drive forward far from men.
While corn is springing from the earth above,
what lies beneath is raked over like a fire,
and out of its rocks comes lapis lazuli,
dusted with flecks of gold.
No bird of prey knows the way there,
and the falcon's keen eye cannot descry it;
proud beasts do not set foot on it,
and no serpent comes that way.

Man sets his hand to the granite rock
and lays bare the roots of the mountains;
he cuts galleries in the rocks,
and gems of every kind meet his eye;
he dams up the sources of the streams
and brings the hidden riches of the earth to light.
But where can wisdom be found?
And where is the source of understanding?
No man knows the way to it;
it is not found in the land of living men.
The depths of ocean say, "It is not in us,"
and the sea says, "It is not with me."
Red gold cannot buy it,
nor can its price be weighed out in silver;
it cannot be set in the scales against gold of Ophir,
against precious cornelian or lapis lazuli;
gold and crystal are not to be matched with it,
no work in fine gold can be bartered for it;
black coral and alabaster are not worth mention,
and a parcel of wisdom fetches more than red coral;
topaz from Ethiopia is not to be matched with it,
it cannot be set in the scales against pure gold.
Where then does wisdom come from,
and where is the source of understanding?
No creature on earth can see it,
and it is hidden from the birds of the air.
Destruction and death say,
"We know of it only by report."
But God understands the way to it,
he alone knows its source;
for he can see to the ends of the earth
and he surveys everything under heaven.
When he made a counterpoise for the wind
and measured out the waters in proportion,
when he laid down a limit for the rain
and a path for the thunderstorm,
even then he saw wisdom and took stock of it,
he considered it and fathomed its very depths.
And he said to man:
    The fear of the Lord is wisdom,
    and to turn from evil is understanding.

(Job 28, NEB)

Now, whom do you judge the speaker to be? It doesn't say. What is the subject? It says that in spite of the stupendous achievements of man, he can't find wisdom. Makes sense, don't you think? But in the last verse there is an answer which sounds like several verses in the book of Proverbs, such as 1:7; 9:10.

Is Job talking? If so, in what a different vein from the preceding! Is Job throwing in the sponge? But chapters 29-31, which follow immediately, don't sound like it.

Is the author preparing us for the mood of Job after God himself has spoken?

It is very difficult to put this magnificent poem into the argument at this point. You may well wish to get the help of a commentary here. But don't fail to read it, with all the exciting references to mining, to precious metals and gems, to birds and streams. And after that, move right into the next chapter.

"... if we want a summary of moral duties from the Old Testament, it might better be found in Job's soliloquy . . . than in the Ten Commandments."

—source unknown.

11. The Shattered Victim's Final Defense!

Here is a possible outline for these three deeply moving chapters, 29—31:

29: The *wonderful* way it used to be.
30: The *unendurable* way it is now!
31: But Job still claims, "I'm an *innocent man!*
Bring on some specific charges!"

Or you might shorten the outline:

29: Look at me then.
30: Look at me now!
31: But you're still looking at an innocent man!

If the opening words of chapter 29 don't draw powerfully on your emotions, what will? Read them aloud from your favorite translation. How can you help admiring this man? See Job sitting there on the village dump pile and note his comment in 30:30; while you see the sights and smell the smells, listen to his voice!

Remember what his friends all said: "You're bad! You're bad! You're bad!!! That's why you're suffering!" And he shouts back, "I'm *not* bad!!!"

(If you are wondering whether Job claims that he is a perfect man, be sure to see the note at the end of this chapter.)

H. Wheeler Robinson used this chart[1] to indicate the varying moods, the terrible ups and downs of Job's feelings.

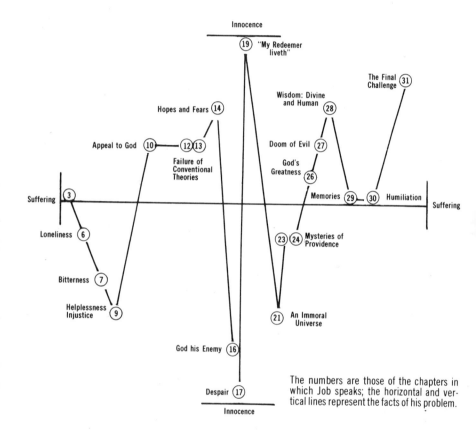

The numbers are those of the chapters in which Job speaks; the horizontal and vertical lines represent the facts of his problem.

[1] H. W. Robinson, *The Cross in the Old Testament* (Philadelphia: The Westminster Press, 1955), p. 14. Used by permission.

See how much you can find in this chart. The figures indicate chapters. The center line seems to be the dividing point between Job's higher and his lower moments. In the chapters indicated above the line he is a bit more hopeful, a bit more confident, has a bit more faith. But in those below, he is more troubled, more nearly hopeless, more depressed, and even more blasphemous. The top and bottom of the chart indicate his innocence. On the left it begins with his suffering and ends on the right with suffering again.

Try making a list of what Job would say:
I am *not* guilty of

Then go on with "I *solemnly swear* that I *have* succeeded in doing the following good deeds in my lifetime":
1)
2)
3)

Can you see his eyes? Are they still flashing (see 15:12), or are they now closed as on page 48 of *Job for Modern Man?*

Chapter 31 represents a very, very high ethical standard. What else can you think of that Job might have done?

We are now ready for a great revealing, a grand climax; but it does not come until chapter 38. In the meantime—

SOME MORE THINGS TO THINK ABOUT

Some people raise the question of whether Job doesn't think of himself as too nearly perfect. As Pope says in *The Anchor Bible,* "...Job vehemently denies that he has sinned, at least not seriously enough to merit such misery as has been inflicted on him."[2] Remember the last part of that and look up 7:21; 10:15; 13:26*b;* 14:17. How good were the "good old days" in your experience? Why do you think Job completely ignores his three friends in these chapters? Or doesn't he? Whom do you believe about Job's past life, Job, or his friends? Why? Does the fact that he makes a most solemn oath about it (31:5-8) influence you? The writer of these lines finds it tremendously impressive.

Do any of Job's words remind you of Joseph Parker's, famous minister of City Temple, London, in another generation, who at the age of 68 said in his suffering, "In that dark hour I became almost an atheist. . . . If I had seen a dog in such agony as mine I would have pitied and helped the dumb beast; yet God spat upon me. . . ."[3]

Excerpt from *Job,* The Anchor Bible, vol. 15, Introduction, Translation, and Notes by Marvin H. Pope (Garden City, N.Y.: Doubleday & Company, Inc., 1973), p. LXX. Reprinted by permission of the publisher.

[3] Joseph Parker, *A Preacher's Life: An Autobiography and an Album* (London: Hodder and Stoughton, Ltd., 1899), p. 211.

68 • if I could find God

Would you like to meet one of the "angry young men"? (32:2)

12. Give Youth a Say!

These lines are being written by a person who is in his later sixties. He is delighted that at this point in the book of Job a young, or at least much younger voice is now heard! Never mind if the voice is at first angry; never mind if it is cocky.

My father once said to me, "John, when you were a college sophomore, you embarrassed me." As I look back on *how much* I thought I knew then, and how I let on openly at times to the fact, I feel that my Dad was greatly understating.

At what point, or points, in *your* life have you felt that you knew a tremendous lot about many things?

Now we are ready to look at Elihu, who was the youngest of all who appear in the pages of the Book of Job (32:4). How old? It does not say. But don't be turned off by 36:4. Be sure to look this up!

Read chapters 32–37 in any translation you choose: six straight chapters from the lips of an angry young man (or does he soften as he goes along?).

Please check the statements about Elihu which correspond to the way you now see him:

courteous
self-confident

bombastic
a poet of outstanding ability
patronizing
cocky
outspoken
really concerned about Job
shy
thoughtful and keen
egotistical
brilliant, well educated
sophomoric
pompous
deeply religious
           or what?

Write down in one or two sentences what Elihu says in his first speech (why does he take so long to get going?): (32, 33)

His second address (34) might be summed up as follows:

Speech number three (35) argues:

And his fourth (36, 37), called the most impressive of the four, says:

How does one size up a biblical character? There must be no snap judgments; so let's live with Elihu for a few days and look at him from all angles. (Perhaps we need to listen more to youth?)

A real biblical student reads between the lines; he doesn't "read stuff in" that is contrary to what's there, but he watches people move, hears their voices in all their varying moods.

We must get help at times when we get stuck. See the one-foot shelf of the most helpful books, on page 109.

Does the following help in your study of Elihu?

WHAT I LIKE MOST ABOUT ELIHU	WHAT I LIKE LEAST ABOUT ELIHU
He desperately wanted to speak up for God. He waited for the older men to speak first.	He was too convinced of his great wisdom and knowledge. He took so long to get under way!

Here without question is some beautiful and powerful poetry. He alone calls Job by name; why didn't the others?

34:36 sounds *just plain cruel!* How sarcastic can one get (34:16)?

You may want to add some more

Now let's give youth its due. Put in one sentence what you think Elihu contributed to the argument. Eliphaz had hinted at it (5:17); Elihu develops it.

God "delivers the afflicted by their affliction, and opens their ear by adversity . . . who is a teacher like him?" (36:15, 22*b*, RSV). God may use adversity and suffering to warn, to discipline, to teach wayward man. This is the educational, not the punitive value of suffering. Can you think of some situation that illustrates this? Take two minutes to think about it.

The February 1, 1960, issue of *Newsweek* carried an exciting article, "Why God Lets Us Suffer." High schoolers reading the United Presbyterian monthly, *Hi Way,* were asked to send in answers. More than a hundred did so, and many of the answers were extremely sensitive. Here is one:

Suffering has a purpose. It makes us think about ourselves and our relationship to God. [1]

You may want to look up this issue in your local library to read the five other penetrating answers which were quoted.

How do you picture Elihu now? The writer of these lines sees him as

[1] "Why God Lets Us Suffer," *Newsweek* (February 1, 1960), p. 80. Copyright Newsweek, Inc., 1960. Reprinted by permission.

perhaps in his thirties. He has a logical mind, a sharp tongue, a real gift of oratory; he is devout, concerned, and has deep theological insights. He can be cruel at times. But in spite of his wordiness, he deserves credit for a real contribution. (Do you agree, or not?) But does this help Job in his suffering? No; for all along he has maintained that he is an innocent man, taking it on the chin far above anything he could possibly deserve.

SOME MORE THINGS TO THINK ABOUT

Have you ever looked up the contributions of famous people before they were thirty? or even twenty-five? Some amazing facts come out. Your local library may contain help on this.

Are you interested in investigating ways in which young people and older people can talk together more naturally about religion? I think we owe our youth today a real debt for making it easier to speak, and reverently, about God and Jesus Christ (see some of the newer religious songs).

Elihu tries to defend God to Job; does God need defenders so much as witnesses?

Many, especially in the past, have questioned the authorship of the Elihu speeches; some writers feel that they add nothing to the argument. The first is, in this book, a purely academic question (this is not a commentary); the second—well, this author feels differently.

The writer of these lines not only prays for the young people of today; but since he represents the older generation he has pasted in the back of his Bible the oft-quoted prayer, written by a nun:

Lord, Thou knowest better than I know myself that I am growing older, and will someday be old.

Keep me from getting talkative, and particularly from the fatal habit of thinking I must say something on every subject and on every occasion.

Release me from craving to try to straighten out everybody's affairs.

Keep my mind free from the recital of endless details. Give me wings to get to the point.

I ask for grace enough to listen to the tales of others' pains. Help me endure them with patience.

But seal my lips on my own aches and pains. They are increasing and my love of rehearsing them is becoming sweeter as the years go by.

Teach me the glorious lesson that occasionally it is possible that I may be mistaken.

Keep me reasonably sweet. I do not want to be a saint—some of them are so hard to live with—but a sour old woman is one of the crowning works of the devil.

Make me thoughtful, but not moody; helpful, but not bossy. With my vast store of wisdom, it seems a pity not to use it all—but Thou knowest, Lord, that I want a few friends at the end.[2]

---

[2] This prayer was written by a Roman Catholic nun. It has had several published appearances.

"The Book of Job is essentially an account of one man's meeting with God. . . ."

—Richard E. Singer [1]

---

[1] Richard E. Singer, *Job's Encounter* (New York: Bookman Associates, imprint of Twayne Publishers, Inc., 1963), p. 8.

13. God Himself Speaks

THE CLIMAX

The first thing, as always, is to read the Scripture passage. Let's try the four chapters, 38-41, in four modern translations. This is the most important section of your study. Do not hurry or skim.

Then the LORD addressed Job out of the storm and said:
Who is this that obscures divine plans with words of
    ignorance?
Gird up your loins now, like a man;
    I will question you, and you tell me the answers!
Where were you when I founded the earth?
    Tell me, if you have understanding.
Who determined its size; do you know?
    Who stretched out the measuring line for it?
Into what were its pedestals sunk,
    and who laid the cornerstone,

While the morning stars sang in chorus
   and all the sons of God shouted for joy?
And who shut within doors the sea,
   when it burst forth from the womb;
When I made the clouds its garment
   and thick darkness its swaddling bands?
When I set limits for it
   and fastened the bar of its door.
And said: Thus far shall you come but no farther,
   and here shall your proud waves be stilled!
Have you ever in your lifetime commanded the morning
   and shown the dawn its place
For taking hold of the ends of the earth,
   till the wicked are shaken from its surface?
The earth is changed as is clay by the seal,
   and dyed as though it were a garment;
But from the wicked the light is withheld,
   and the arm of pride is shattered.

Have you entered into the sources of the sea,
   or walked about in the depths of the abyss?
Have the gates of death been shown to you,
   or have you seen the gates of darkness?
Have you comprehended the breadth of the earth?
   Tell me, if you know all:
Which is the way to the dwelling place of light,
   and where is the abode of darkness,
That you may take them to their boundaries
   and set them on their homeward paths?
You know, because you were born before them,
   and the number of your years is great!

Have you entered the storehouse of the snow,
   and seen the treasury of the hail
Which I have reserved for times of stress,

for the days of war and of battle?
Which way to the parting of the winds,
   whence the east wind spreads over the earth?

Who has laid out a channel for the downpour
   and for the thunderstorm a path
To bring rain to no man's land,
   the unpeopled wilderness;
To enrich the waste and desolate ground
   till the desert blooms with verdure?

Has the rain a father;
   or who has begotten the drops of dew?
Out of whose womb comes the ice,
   and who gives the hoarfrost its birth in the skies,
When the waters lie covered as though with stone
   that holds captive the surface of the deep?

Have you fitted a curb to the Pleiades,
   or loosened the bonds of Orion?
Can you bring forth the Mazzaroth in their season,
   or guide the Bear with its train?
Do you know the ordinances of the heavens;
   can you put into effect their plan on the earth?

Can you raise your voice among the clouds,
   or veil yourself in the waters of the storm?
Can you send forth the lightnings on their way,
   or will they say to you, "Here we are"?
Who counts the clouds in his wisdom?
   Or who tilts the water jars of heaven
So that the dust of earth is fused into a mass
   and its clods made solid?
Do you hunt the prey for the lioness
   or appease the hunger of her cubs,

While they crouch in their dens,
    or lie in wait in the thicket?
Who puts wisdom in the heart,
    and gives the cock its understanding?
Who provides nourishment for the ravens
    when their young ones cry out to God,
and they rove abroad without food? (Job 38, *The New American Bible*)

Do you know how wild goats breed, upon the hills?
    Can you control the calving of the hinds?
Do you fix their appointed time?
    Do you know when they are to bear?
Down they bend, and the womb opens,
    as they drop their young—
lusty offspring, thriving in the open,
    that run off and return not to the herd.

Who gave the wild ass his freedom?
    Who let the swift ass roam at large,
whose home I make the steppes,
    whose dwelling is the salty land?
He scorns the noisy town,
    ,he hears no driver's shout;
he scours the hills for pasture,
    in search of any green thing.

Will the wild ox be content to slave for you?
Will he stay in your stable?
Can you rope him to your plow?
    Will he harrow the furrows for you?
Will you trust to his tremendous strength,
    and let him do your fieldwork?
Will you rely on him to come
    and carry corn home to your threshing-floor?

Do you supply the war-horse with his strength,
or cover his neck with the tossing mane?
Do you make him leap forward like a locust,
snorting bravely, furiously?
He paws the valley proudly,
facing the clash of arms;
he mocks at fear, unterrified,
he flies not from the sword;
the quiver rattles against him,
the glittering spear and javelin,
but on he charges in wild rage,
straight ahead, never swerving;
the trumpet sounds—"Aha!" he cries,
scenting the battle from afar,
where captains thunder, 'mid the shouts of war.

Does your wit send the hawk to soar
and spread her wings for the south?
Does your word make the eagle mount
to nest aloft among the hills?
Her home is high upon the cliffs,
on the peak of the crag she perches;
she spies her prey from the height,
with eyes that see from far;
her young ones suck up blood,
and where the slain are, there is she.
((The ostrich flaps her wings in pride;
but is the feathered creature kind?
She leaves her eggs upon the earth
to warm and hatch out in the dust,
forgetting that a foot may crush them,
or a wild beast tread on them—
harsh to her young, as if they were not hers,
unheeding though her labour is in vain;
for God makes her devoid of sense,

God Himself Speaks • 83

he denies her intelligence.
Let hunters come, and she will scour the plain,
   scorning the horse and its rider.)) (Job 39, A New Translation,
   Moffatt)

   Then the LORD answered Job, saying:
"Will the fault-finder argue with the Almighty?
He who chides God, let him answer for it."
(Then follow three verses in the mouth of Job.)
Then the LORD answered Job from the tempest, saying:
"Gird up your loins, now, like a man;
I will ask you, and do you instruct me.
Will you, indeed, break down my right?
Will you make me guilty that you may be innocent?
Or have you an arm like God,
And can you thunder with a voice like his?
Deck yourself, now, with majesty and eminence,
And clothe yourself with glory and splendor.
Scatter abroad the rage of your wrath;
And look upon everyone that is proud and abase him.
Look upon everyone who is proud and bring him low;
And crush the wicked where they stand.
Bury them in the dust likewise;
Bind up their faces in the hidden place.
Then I indeed will praise you,
That your own right hand can deliver you.

"Behold, now, the hippopotamus which I made along with
   you;
He eats grass like the ox.
Behold, now, his strength in his loins,
And his might in the muscles of his body.
He stiffens his tail like a cedar;
The sinews of his thighs are knit together.
His bones are tubes of bronze;

His limbs are like bars of iron.
He is the chief of the ways of God;
Let him who made him bring near his sword!
For the mountains bring him their produce,
And all the beasts of the field play there.
Beneath the lotus bushes he lies down,
In the depths of reed and swamp.
The lotus bushes screen him as his shade;
The willows of the brook surround him.
If the river press upon him, he is not disturbed;
He is confident when the Jordan swells to his mouth.
Can one seize him by his eyes?
Can one pierce his nose with traps?'' (Job 40, *An American Translation*)

Can you draw out the crocodile with a hook or hold down his tongue with a cord? Can you put a rush line through his gills or pierce his jaw with a spur? Will he make repeated requests of you? Will he use friendly words in addressing you? Will he make a bargain with you, that you should take him as your servant for life? Will you play with him as with a bird or keep him as a plaything for your girls? Will fishermen traders bargain over him, apportioning him among the merchants? Can you fill his skin with barbed darts or his head with harpoons? Lay your hand upon him; then remember the conflict; you will not do it a second time! The man who hopes to master him will be disillusioned; at the sight of him a person is paralyzed! No one is foolhardy enough to stir him up; who then is he who can stand before Me? From whom have I borrowed, that I should have to repay him? Every thing under the whole heaven is Mine.

I will not be silent concerning his limbs, his mighty strength and his artistic proportions. Who has ever stripped off his thick coat of mail, or pierced his impenetrable scales? Who can open the doors of his mouth? Around his teeth there is terror. His back is shingled with scales, as closely fitted together as a tight seal. So near are his scales to one another that no air can get between them. They clasp one another, joined so closely they cannot be separated. His sneezings sparkle light; his eyes are like the rays of morning. Out of his jaws come burning torches, and sparks of fire shoot out. From his nostrils vapor issues as steam from a boiling pot over burning rushes. His breath sets coals on fire; a flame issues from his mouth. Such strength dwells in his neck that panic moves before him. The folds of his flesh close in on each other, firmly and immovably cast upon him. His heart is as hard as a rock; solid as a nether millstone. When he raises himself up, the mighty are afraid; beside themselves with panic. To hit him with a sword is useless; so with a spear, a dart, or a javelin. To him iron is as straw and copper as rotten wood. Arrows do not rout him; slingstones he treats as stubble. Clubs are counted by him as reeds, and he mocks the rattle of javelins. His nether parts are like potsherds; they leave threshing-sledge grooves in the mire. He makes the deep to boil as a pot, the sea like a vessel of ointment. Behind him he leaves a foaming wake; one wonders if the sea might be growing hoary! On earth there is not his equal, a creature devoid of fear! He looks down on all that is high; he is king over all the sons of pride. (Job 41, The Modern Language Bible, *Berkeley Version)*

**Write down a quick reaction to these speeches
of God himself.**

Now go back to the beginning of the awe-inspiring setting. What is the weather like? "Then out of the storm, the Lord spoke to Job" (Job 38:1, *Today's English Version*). Try reading it in various ways:

"Then *out of the storm,* the Lord spoke to Job."

"Then out of the storm, *the Lord* spoke to Job."

"Then out of the storm, the Lord spoke *to Job.*"

Do you begin to see all that is in this verse?

Why did God confront Job in a heavy storm? Try to visualize the scene as far as is humanly possible. (See other cases in the Old Testament when a meeting between God and man took place under similar conditions: 2 Kings 2:1, 11; Isaiah 29:6; Jeremiah 23:19; 25:32; 30:23; Ezekiel 1:4; 13:11; Amos 1:14, for example. But compare this with 1 Kings 19:11, 12!) Under what physical circumstances has God come into *your* life with some kind of message?

Now think for a few minutes of the speeches as a whole. In an English novel by Charles Williams, *War in Heaven,* one minister, during a conversation on suffering, says to another clergyman, "As a mere argument there's something lacking perhaps in saying to a man who's lost his money and his house and his family and is sitting on the dustbin, all over boils, 'Look at the hippopotamus.'" [2]

Suppose for a moment that you could have taken the place of the inspired writer of the Book of Job. Write below what you would feel that God would say to a good man who had "taken it on the chin" the way Job had. Do you wonder why the answer of God wasn't more comforting? Or might he have said something about Job's fine character? Would there possibly well have been a word of forgiveness? Or some other form of reproof than the one which we find here? Take a few minutes on this.

[2] Charles Williams, *War in Heaven* (New York: Pellegrini & Cudahy, 1949; now Farrar, Straus & Giroux, Inc.), p. 22.

Consider the following statements and see if they help in your study of this section. See, too, if you agree with them.

God's silence was at last broken.

Job got what he had asked for so insistently—a face-to-face confrontation.

But it came in an entirely different form from what he had expected!

It showed him that there were vast areas about which he knew nothing.

God did not condemn him for his past life.

Yet the sarcasm was very devastating to his ego.

There were no answers of the kind Job had hoped for.

Job learned that God is always there, and at work, regardless of whether Job might be aware of him, or not.

How remarkable that a God who is behind such a universe could care enough about a mere man to have a meeting with, and a message for him!

Job learned that he was no equal of God, that he could not stand up to him and make demands.

Now look quickly at chapters 40 and 41. Ask questions:

Is this a real, an oversized, or an imaginary hippopotamus and crocodile? Check the details carefully.

Look up the habits of the two powerful beasts in your public library. You will find many fascinating pictures and details.

How did the author know so much about them?

Why were these two chosen, and not, say, the lion and the elephant?

What wild beasts were best known in the area in which this great writing originated (but there is disagreement as to what that area was!)?

Then turn back to chapters 38 and 39, and talk back to these powerful questions.

Why was God so sarcastic? What do you think the place of sarcasm is in life?

Make a list of all the animals and birds mentioned here.

Then list the constellations of stars talked about, so far as we can tell which ones are referred to. *Today's English Version* has some helpful suggestions in the footnotes.

You may find that you have many, many questions about these four chapters. Many do. Hold them, mull them over at odd times during the day and evening. Do not make up your mind finally about them until you have gone through the next chapter of this book. In that chapter we shall see the effect of God's speeches on Job.

A GREAT SERMON ON JOB

Theodore Parker Ferris, beloved rector of Trinity Church, Boston, Massachusetts, died prematurely in 1972 of a malignant disease. Some years before, he had preached four very striking sermons, "Job Among the Ashes," "Job and His Friends," "Job and His Religion," and "Job and God." About a month before he passed on, Dr. Ferris in a personal letter graciously granted the present writer the right to use "anything you want to include in your book on Job. . . ." Accordingly, a part of the final sermon of the series now follows. It greatly illuminates many of the matters raised in this chapter.

When a man rages against God, his rage at the very least is a sign of this, that he still believes there is a God to rage against. So the sickness of disgust may be the dark side of the moon, and the moon may turn. It often does. It did for Job. For finally, God spoke to Job. After what must have seemed an interminable length of time, God spoke to Job, not face to face but, as the poet says, "out of the whirlwind." Not out of just an ordinary storm, a spring shower, but out of a cataclysmic hurricane, the kind which man used to imagine would end the world.

Out of that storm God spoke to Job, and the first thing to notice is what He did not say. It is striking and surprising when you stop to think of it. He never referred to, or even mentioned, Job's suffering, either to explain it or to soothe it. Doesn't that surprise you? After all that Job had been through, you might have expected God to say, "Now you've had a tough time of it, and you have done well. Keep your chin up. Things will be better." He never mentioned it.

He never answered any of the questions Job had asked. We have been thinking about Job for three Sundays, and we have talked about some of the questions with which Job lashed the skies. Why didn't I die when I was born? What have I done wrong? What has God against me? Why do the wicked prosper? God never made the slightest attempt to answer any of these questions.

Neither did He say anything about Job's behavior, good or bad, past or present, and this had been the subject of the whole poem. It was the thing that concerned both Job and his friends, for upon it depended his religious future. God never mentioned it. Nor did He say a word about Job's questioning His motive or doubting His goodness. He didn't condemn him; He didn't say, You have been bold and brash to raise questions about the justice of my ways. Not a word. And He never attempted to justify His own actions or to condemn Job's.

The first thing He said was this: (I am paraphrasing this in the hope that it may make a fresh impact upon you, the way it did upon Job) God said, Stand up like a man and answer my questions. In other words, *God didn't pity Job. He challenged him.* There are times when the right thing to do is to go down into the ashes with another person and sympathize with him. And we who know the mystery of the Cross know that there are times when God does that very thing. But there are other times when human beings in their suffering are so filled with self-pity that the thing to do is what God did with Job, and that is to speak rather sternly to him, and say, "Gird up now thy loins like a man; for I will demand of thee, and answer thou me."

Then He began asking him questions, and they are all embarrassing questions because the answer to all was, in one way or another, No. You remember them, and I hesitate again to paraphrase them because the English of the King James Version is so incredibly beautiful, and yet once again I think that to get the impact of them, it would be better if I did. These are some of the questions that God asked Job.

Were you there when I laid the foundations of the earth? No. Can you bind up the Pleiades in a cluster, or loose the chains of Orion? No. Can you count the clouds? No. Can you feed the ravens? No. Did you give the peacocks their wings? No. Have you given the horse his strength? No. Do you set off the lightning? No. Do you tilt the pitchers of the sky? No. Does the eagle fly at your command? No. Have you ever roused the morning or given directions to the dawn? No.

And so it goes, on and on, and all the questions seem to be calculated to make Job feel small. You know how you feel if you are being examined by someone and you don't know the answers to any of the questions. If you haven't an inferiority complex already, you soon will have and, in passing, I think we can say that the next thing worse to feeling sinful is to feel small, to feel yourself shrinking in significance. And on first reading, and perhaps in some cases on second and third reading, this seems a heartless procedure on the part of God. If you saw a big man making a small man feel smaller than he already is, you would say that man is a mean man, wouldn't you? And a great many people are inclined to say that it is mean on the part of God to make Job feel so small.

But the fact is, you see, that the questions with their negative answers didn't make Job feel small at all, really. They made him feel *alive* again. As the questions were flung at Job one after the other, it was as though his life was coming back. I thought of the way a doctor slaps a baby when he is born to get the breathing started, and the effects of this long examination on the part of God seemed to me something like that. It made Job feel humble, of course; but it didn't make him feel small and insignificant. It made him come alive again.

Yes, the moon was turning. The other side of the darkness was beginning to appear, and our question is, Why? How did it happen? What was there about this experience that would do that to a person? Here let me say parenthetically that we are on difficult ground because all we can do is proceed by the use of our own imagination, limited as it is. I have tried to do this in a way that will be fair to the experience of Job, and also perhaps enlighten here and there your own experience.

The first thing that I have put down as an attempt to answer the question, Why does this particular kind of experience do what we have said it did for Job, is this: God's examination of Job began to make Job think of something else besides himself. As God kept asking those questions that had nothing to do with Job, nothing to do with his suffering, nothing to do with his family or his aches and pains, nothing to do with his questions or problems, Job found his attention being turned away from himself to something quite outside himself. He found himself gradually, wonder of wonders, sharing in the work of creation. His interest was captivated by the wonder and variety of it, as God asked those amazing questions about everything from stars to peacocks.

Do you remember enough about those two great chapters to remember that after God talked to him about the creation and all that it implied, He then began talking to him about the animals? Can you imagine anything more ironical than talking to somebody who is in the depths of trouble about the animal life of the world? He talked to him about the goats and the way they brought forth their young; and the wild asses, how they couldn't bear living in the cities but roamed the open plains, even though they had to work hard to get enough to eat; about the unicorns and the peacocks; and the ostrich with his fleetness, more swift even than the horse; and then the horses, and the hawks; the hippopotamus and the whale.

I have known a man to recover his sanity by getting an interest in birds and watching them so closely that he forgot himself. And I have never known anybody to have a healthy sense of the meaningfulness of life who hadn't had some experience which drew him entirely out of his preoccupation with his aches and pains, problems and questions, and all the other things that so often concern him. That is the first thing, then, to say about Job's experience, and yours.

The next is this. As God fired question after question at him, Job began to realize that he didn't know as much as he thought he did. He discovered in this examination what some people, I am afraid, even in this day and age when we have so much material to help us, never discover. He finally came to see that he was completely surrounded by vast margins of mystery. He knew as he had never known before that there were some questions he would never know the answers to.

A man who spends his life studying the stars is not likely to be sick and disgusted because he can't understand the reason for his own suffering. He is too well acquainted with mystery to think that he can reduce the mystery of human suffering to a mathematical formula that he can grasp with his own little mind. On the other hand, the man who thinks he knows all the answers, and there are many, especially—I am afraid—within the bounds of conventional religion, the man who thinks he knows all the answers is the man who has, or is likely to have, no answer when he loses the child who is the most precious thing in his life. All his neatly-constructed theories fall with a crash to the ground.

This is one of the mysteries, and I do not want to press it too far. I hope that you are reading Job's experience into your own life and are conducting a private examination right now to discover whether you are one of those who have thought all along that you knew everything there was to know about life, and that your religion gave you all the answers, ready-made, and therefore human suffering, whenever and however it overtook you, would present no mystery at all. If you are that kind of person, immerse yourself in the mystery in which Job found himself completely wrapped.

Another thing is this, and this came to me for the first time as I read the Book of Job getting ready for these sermons. Job saw God for the first time quite apart from himself and his own needs. That makes a difference. Job, like many prosperous people, many pious people, good people like you, had invariably thought of God as the One from whom all blessings flow. They had flowed, with almost miraculous abundance, straight to him, and that was great, and God was great! But when they stopped flowing, that wasn't so great, and God wasn't so great. But now he saw God Himself, quite apart from the blessings. It was as though he saw God yearning over His creation the way a mother yearns over her child, remembering perhaps with some nostalgia how the morning stars sang together and the sons of God shouted for joy before things began to go wrong. And Job began to think of God and to see God in Himself quite apart from anything he needed from Him, or from anything that God could do for him, the way a child suddenly sees his parent. For a long time he thinks of his parent almost entirely in terms of himself, what his parent can do for him when he is in trouble, how he can meet his needs, how he can satisfy his pleasures; and then a crisis comes and he hears his father and mother talking in the next room. They don't know that he hears them, or that he suddenly realizes that they have their troubles too, that they are people like himself. From that time on he has an entirely new and more mature relationship with them.

You and I will never be spiritually mature until we can say something like what an unknown Spaniard said in the seventeenth century:

> My God, I love thee; not because
> I hope for heav'n thereby,
> Nor yet for fear that loving not
> I might forever die;
> But as thyself hast loved me,
> O ever-loving Lord!
> E'en so I love thee, and will love,
> And in thy praise will sing,
> Solely because thou art my God
> And my eternal King.

Strangely enough, this isn't quite the end—almost, but not quite. As so often happens, when Job stopped thinking about himself and began to think about God, he knew for the first time, as he never had before, that God was thinking about him, even though He didn't seem to be paying any attention to the things that were immediately troubling him. He knew that God was thinking about him, not in the old way, as one of his favorites that He was helping along, but in a new way, as one whom He had taken into His confidence, one with whom He was sharing some of the problems and joys of creation, assuming that he could handle his own human problems. Which he proceeded to do, of course. Once Job was convinced that God had not forgotten him, that He took the trouble to speak to him, and draw him into his own divine activities, he was sick and disgusted no longer.

Now there is just this to be said. Not once is the word 'love' mentioned, but a man would have to be blind not to see the love of God turning the moon around and around until the dark side was completely hidden again. We do not presume to plumb the depths of this experience and, if we should meditate upon it again in ten or twenty years, we still would not reach the heights or the depths of it. And we do not intend to offer to you who are raising questions about the fairness of life an answer for a song.

All we can say is this. The meaningfulness of life does not come by way of the understanding, only. It comes with the willingness to be, to live, to suffer, to lose, to die. What happened to Job was that this willingness to be, which he had almost completely lost, suddenly returned. He 'saw' something. What he said was, "I have heard of Thee by the hearing of the ear, but now mine eye seeth Thee." What did he see? We shall never know, exactly. But I like to think that he saw, as we see the light of a distant star, the light of the glory of God as it finally shone in the face of Jesus Christ. He never saw the fact itself, but I like to think that in some way not understood by us, the light from it shone backward as well as forward, and that by that light he saw God.

O God, help us to be quiet here in the presence of thy majesty and power and love, the fullness of which we shall never understand, but the reality of which is never beyond our reach. Amen.

One of my students once wrote, "God cut Job down to size." Is that what is happening in this chapter?

14. What Job Said Then

You don't need to read much this time—just eight verses, of which only seven are Job's (and some of those repeat the divine questions). Read, in any translation, 40:3-5; 42:2-6.

Write in your own words what Job says in 40:4, 5. This is his negative response.

What mood do you find expressed most clearly here? Humility? Or what? Take a few moments to think about the exact meaning of the words.

Verses 2-6 in chapter 42 go further. Put *this* also in your own words. This is the positive response.

Here is reverence, repentance, recantation. Do you agree? Anything more? Yes, there is. What?

Notice that Job's shouts have quieted to a whisper. Has that ever happened to you?

Before we move quickly into the next chapter, ask yourself what is it that Job repents of? This is most important. One commentator calls it "theological insolence." Isn't it that Job had talked back to God as an equal, sort of "eyeball to eyeball," accusing the deity of being unmoved by principles of justice although he certainly was all powerful?

In the next chapter we shall see how much was really happening here to Job.

15. Is the End of the Book the Solution?

We always look forward to the last chapter of a book, because that's where the tangled skeins get unraveled. So, you are ready now for Job 42:7-17—eleven verses—but after you've read them, you may be very puzzled!

Don't hurry as you read this section. Let's say again, read between the lines; ask questions; talk back. How much in these verses comes to you as a surprise? Anything? It would help you if you would read it in three different translations. In the author's experience the reading of many versions has increased his understanding of the text very greatly.

Jot down a dozen or so questions that now come to mind, such as:

1. Does it say explicity that Job got well? Why do you think it doesn't?
2. Are you surprised by the last part of verses 7 and 8? (Be sure to read them!)
3. Why isn't "the Satan" mentioned again?
4. Where had the friends and relatives in verse 11 been when Job was so sick?
   (And if you can't fill in the rest, then you haven't really read the passage.)

5.

6.

7.

8.

9.

10.

11.

12.

You see what Paul Scherer meant when he said, "The book of Job is not for the casual reader."[1]

Now move along to the question, does chapter 42:7-17 furnish the solution to the central problem of the book?

But exactly what do you now think *is* the central problem of the book? Here is where different writers have different views. Don't let this worry you too much! Who said the Bible is an easy book to understand? But God gave us brains to use! And after faithful study you can make up your own mind on most of these questions.

If the central problem of the book is, "Will a person keep his faith without material rewards (1:11) and physical well-being (2:4, 5)?" then the answer is that Job never lost his faith in God, but he certainly raised a lot of questions about him. But never for a minute did he say, "I no longer believe in a God!"

If the central problem is, "Yes, God is all-powerful, but is he just?" then the answer seems to be that Job comes to feel he can trust him even if he doesn't in any way understand his way of running the universe.

If the problem is the relation of God and man, and whether God is man's friend or enemy, then we seem to learn here only that man should not try to cut God down to his own size and talk back to him about this as an equal. "Let God be God!"

If it is, "Why does a good God allow good people to suffer so much?" then should we read 42:7-17 as saying, "If the good person

[1] Paul Scherer, "The Book of Job," *The Interpreter's Bible,* ed. George A. Buttrick, et al. (Nashville: Abingdon Press, 1954), vol. 3, p. 1192.

will just hang on and keep believing as much as he can (even if he doesn't understand why he is suffering), then God will make up for all the agony by giving him back as much as he had before and more"? Let's really think hard about this. If you take this as the absolute, unconditional, universal solution of the problem, then you've undone most of that which has gone on in the preceding chapters! The three friends had suggested that coming back to God would ensure a quick return to material prosperity where everything is rosy (5:8ff., 11:13ff.), and most of us haven't thought they were telling it like it is! And now the Almighty seems to clinch it by saying that the three friends *didn't* tell the truth about him (42:7*b*, 8*b*).

In your observation, *does* God reward all your friends who hang on in the midst of their troubles; does he reward them with all they had before and more? How many can you think of who have had such good fortune?

Further, is it possible that an earlier verse in the chapter contains a deeper, more truthful solution or at least suggestion? See what you think of verse 5. Read it aloud several times. The present writer finds that this verse brings a deep and satisfying answer to some of one's deepest yearnings in the midst of suffering. Could it be that what we should hear is the following: A personal experience of God is worth more than any answer to our agonized "why?"

Another consideration lends weight to this use of verse 5 as the central idea of the book: the book returns after the next verse to prose (usually designated "The Prose Epilogue"). This matches the prose we had in the Prologue (chapters 1, 2). Many regard the prose sections as an older framework for the brilliant poetical masterpiece.[2] The fact that the Targum (paraphrase in Aramaic) of Job, a very ancient piece found at Qumran, ends with verse 11 shows that there was some variation in the ending of the book at an early date.

What is the real climax of this book? The present writer hopes that you will work out your own answer. (See the list of helpful books on page 109 if you wish.)

[2] Such a supposition helps greatly in explaining the radical change in Job's mood between chapters 2 and 3.

It may help to raise the question, "Suppose *you* were God and were creating a world of people, what kind of place would you make?" Suppose, now, that you established an earth on which everyone had just exactly what he wanted, and just when he wanted it. What kind of world would this be? Wouldn't the inhabitants be a bunch of spoiled brats? Do not pain and suffering play a part in the making of the characters of some of the finest people you've known? Some of the greatest men and women I've known have grown through trouble into the wonderful people they are today.

Following is the true story of Billy Weatherford. How do you react to it?

When Billy Weatherford was sixteen, he wrote this prayer: "Dear Father, why do I have to be the way I am? Why can't I walk like the other guys I know? Why can't I get out and have fun like other people do? Why does everything seem to be just out of reach?" Why did Billy write such a prayer? He is a cripple and has to stay in a wheelchair. He had polio.

Dr. Allen DuMont, president of the DuMont Laboratories, wrote to Billy and said:

"Dear Billy: I asked myself the same question forty years ago when I was a little younger than you—eleven. Perhaps you like sports. I did. One day I came home from school aching all over. It was polio. The doctors feared I never would walk again. It didn't seem fair that this should happen to me, but what I am most thankful for is that I didn't quit. One day my parents brought me some radio equipment, a few crystals, and a microphone. That was back in 1913 when radio was just a gadget. The stuff fascinated me, and at the end of my year in bed I had built my own radio set. Now, here is the important thing. I might never have become interested in radio if I had not been stricken with polio. During this period my mother prayed for me night and day. I came out with a limp that has been with me all my life, but my energies were then centered on radio, which was the best thing that could have happened to me."

Billy Weatherford, like Allen DuMont, learned to live with his paralysis. He impresses everyone with his good disposition and his searching mind. He loves music and wears braces on his arms while learning to play. Thus he is slowly developing the use of his hands. He also writes poems and is active in church school and church. One day

he said to his mother, "I'd rather be a good Christian than walk."[3]
Take some time and think about the various angles of this true story.

The question still is: Even granted that suffering may well have a place, why do some wonderful people get such a dose of it? We come back to the statement, "A personal experience of God is worth more than any answer." As P. T. Forsyth suggested, Job didn't find the answer but he found the answerer! And alienation from God had been his chief problem (how modern that sounds!). But that was all swept out to sea when his greatest experience finally came!

Years ago a driver at the wheel of a heavily loaded truck crashed head on into a similarly loaded vehicle in the Midwest. The trucker was in an Indiana hospital for weeks. Listen to his amazing words to a minister who visited him: "In my trouble I called on God. He was so real and so near to me, it seemed I could just put out my hand and take hold of his. I would be willing to go through twice the suffering I did, for the comfort I received. . . ."[4]

The presence of evil does not mean the absence of God! We must not end our study of the suffering of Job without letting the shadow of the cross fall across it! For there was agonized suffering by the One who *least* deserved it, but see what God has done through the centuries with that cross! As Hugh Anderson wrote, "The Most High God is to be found in unexpected ways and places, and none more unexpected than Golgotha, the place of a skull, where there is neither comfort nor security but a great agony, where Jesus of Nazareth is crucified and God may be met in his grace and truth."[5]

SOME MORE THINGS TO THINK ABOUT

Let's be honest; the Book of Job contains no answer to the problem of suffering. Does it? So you say, "Then all this study is wasted!" Oh no! There is something here which is better than a solution: The

[3] Quoted in "Hosea, the Loving Husband," *Junior High Topic,* April–May, 1956, p. 17.
[4] William Goulooze, "Meditation of 'The Day of Trouble,'" *Intelligencer-Leader* (January 23, 1935), p. 9.
[5] Charles M. Laymon, ed., *The Interpreter's One-Volume Commentary on the Bible* (Nashville: Abingdon Press, 1971), p. 252.

presence of the one who has the answers! So, we have clues for meeting the problem rather than what we had hoped for; we are better off!

Why do you think the Satan is not mentioned again? Is it because he has been defeated? Or why?

Be sure to study Job's intercessory prayer for his three friends. How much of your prayer is this kind?

Why is there special mention of the fact that the beautiful daughters in the new family inherited part of Job's tremendous estate along with the brothers?

Notice that the Book of Job does not handle such questions as, Aren't there two kinds of evil—man-made and God-caused? It assumes that God being omnipotent is ultimately responsible. We are inclined to say today that we certainly cannot blame God for all the suffering and pain we see. Yet who allowed cancer to come into the world? However, we must add that he has given man great powers in conquering or at least alleviating disease. So we feel that he allows pain and suffering in a world where his ultimate object, we believe, is the making of character, Christian character.

Also, the book does not handle all the hazards of human free will. If you'd been God, would you have allowed man so much of it?

Are you interested in discovering, in other Near Eastern literature, writings dealing with some of the problems we have been facing in the Book of Job? Pope in the introduction of his commentary[6] prints excerpts from such poems as the Egyptian "Dispute Over Suicide," "Tale of the Eloquent Peasant," and the Babylonian "Poem of the Righteous Sufferer"; he also tells the story of "Prometheus Bound." Writers in other cultures have wrestled with these problems in varying ways. In modern times Goethe's *Faust,* H. G. Wells' *The Undying Fire,*[7] Robert Frost's "A Masque of Reason,"[8] and

---

[6]*Job,* The Anchor Bible, vol. 15, Introduction, Translation, and Notes by Marvin H. Pope (Garden City, N. Y.: Doubleday & Company, Inc., 1973), pp. L-LXVII.

[7]H. G. Wells, *The Undying Fire* (New York: The Macmillan Company, 1919).

[8]Robert Frost, "A Masque of Reason" *Complete Poems of Robert Frost* (New York: Holt, Rinehart & Winston, Inc., 1948).

Archibald MacLeish's *J. B.,*[9] demonstrate that the agonies of the world are perennial.

Leslie Weatherhead, the well-known preacher for years at City Temple, London, and one of the pioneers in the area of pastoral psychology, has a paperback entitled, *Why Do Men Suffer?*[10] with some penetrating suggestions and powerful illustrations. And Wesley Baker has done a very commendable job in his *More Than a Man Can Take,* also in a paperback edition.[11]

[9] Archibald MacLeish, *J. B.* (Boston: Houghton Mifflin Company, 1958).
[10] Leslie D. Weatherhead, *Why Do Men Suffer?* (Nashville: Abingdon Press, 1936).
[11] Wesley Baker, *More Than a Man Can Take* (Philadelphia: Westminster Press, 1966).

Postscript:
The Hardest Things About the Book of Job: A Few Suggestions

One difficulty which so many of us have here is that it's very hard to get final answers to some of our deepest problems. Do you feel frustrated now that you have finished your study of the Book of Job? Did you expect to get a lot of clear-cut explanations to the question of human suffering? Perhaps we'll have to wait a bit for some of these.

Another frustration is the way certain verses are translated in different versions. If the translation in one is right, then the other or others are all off. Don't the translators know what they are doing, you ask? Can't they agree? Well, the answer is that many times the Hebrew text of Job is not only difficult, but it's unclear. See, for example, the difference in the *King James Version* and *The Living Bible* rendering of Job 13:15!

Also, the Book of Job is hard because the speeches are so long-winded and so many in number. Or don't you feel this way?

Finally, we feel frustrated when the commentaries differ so widely on important passages. This is true (because the text is hard) of such a very great passage as 19:23-27. How much of a glimpse of another life did the hero have? This is worth considerable study.

Yet in the preceding pages we have presented many, many things about which there is little or no doubt! And as for the rest, suspend your judgment for the time being and keep working until new light comes. For, as Pastor Robinson said to the embarking Pilgrims, "... I am confident that God hath more truth yet to break forth out of His Holy Word."

Appendix:
Brief Explanation of 25 Hard Terms

(as used in the *Revised Standard Version*)

Abaddon (26:6): another name for Sheol, the place of all the dead. The word means "destruction."

Bear (9:9; 38:32): the constellation which contains the Big Dipper. The identification of some of the star groups in the Book of Job is not certain.

Behemoth (40:15): a hippopotamus-like monster.

Buzite (32:2): the name of a clan (see Gen. 22:21) or Aramean tribe.

Jemimah (42:14): one of Job's new daughters; it means "dove."

Keren-happuch (42:14): another daughter; means "box for eye makeup."

Keziah (42:14): the third daughter; means "cassia" or "cinnamon."

Leviathan (41:1): a crocodile-like monster. (In 3:8 the reference is to a sea monster, dating back to primeval times, still threatening the created order.)

Mazzaroth (38:32): undoubtedly a constellation, but identification is difficult.

Onyx (28:16): precious stone with layers of color; but exact identification of the Hebrew word is not certain.

Ophir (22:24): location unsure; South Arabia?

Orion (38:31): constellation easily picked out by the belt and sword.

Pillars (of the earth) (9:6): in the cosmology of the day, the boundaries of the earth sat on pillars which held it up over primeval water.

Pit (33:24): same as Sheol, place of all the dead.

Pleiades (38:31): constellation sometimes known as "The Seven Sisters."

Purslane (6:6): a plant with a fleshy stem which exudes something like mucilage. The identification is not certain, but there is clear reference to something terribly flat and insipid.

Rahab (9:13): usually identified with a primeval dragon-like monster which had been overcome by the deity at the beginning of the era.

Ram (32:2): a clan name.

Redeemer (19:25): the Hebrew word means the next of kin, whose duty it was to redeem family property, or avenge the spilling of family blood, or raise children for a childless brother. The Book of Ruth gives an illustration of the first. Job is not asking to be redeemed from Sheol but to be vindicated before men. "Vindicator" is used here in some of the translations. The word stands in a series of verses which are not only unusually hard to translate because of a difficult text (a literal word-by-word translation doesn't make very much sense in this verse) but are also at least a momentary breakthrough in Job's tortured thinking. Several commentaries might well be used here.

Sapphire (28:6, 16): a precious stone, ordinarily blue. Some translate the Hebrew word "lapis lazuli," an azure-blue, semiprecious combination of minerals.

Satan (1:6 and following): better, "The Satan," since the Hebrew has the definite article each time in this book. He is portrayed here as a supernatural being, member of God's heavenly court, a sort of watchdog and prosecutor who checks on humans and reports to God.

Sheol (11:8): the place where all the dead go, good and bad alike. See Job's words about it in 10:21, 22, for example.

Sons of God (1:6 and following): the heavenly court, made up of superhuman beings carrying out God's directives.

Topaz (28:19): a semiprecious stone, ordinarily yellow in color. The Hebrew word may mean yellow chrysolite.

Umpire (9:33): here, not one who makes a decision, but a go-between, a conciliator, "who might lay his hand upon us both."

A Twelve-Inch Shelf of the Most Helpful Books

In case you'd like further help on the Book of Job let's suggest a small shelf of books to which you can go back again and again. You may wish to substitute other titles; the books listed have helped many lay people on some of the difficult points. There is room at the end of the list for you to add others.

First of all on your shelf there should be a translation of the whole Bible in the language of today. Why? We say again that the *King James Version* (1611) is the most beautiful one you'll ever read; but you need a translation in today's understandable English. Many of you use the *Revised Standard Version;* let's assume the presence of this helpful work; but put a more colloquial (in the best sense) translation on your special shelf. You may want to choose one of these; all are in paperback editions; they are listed alphabetically:

The Jerusalem Bible (1966)

The Living Bible (1971)

The New American Bible (1970)

The New English Bible (1961)

It would help to have, in addition, a pocket edition of Job that you can carry around and read while waiting. Choose one:

"Tried and True:" *Job for Modern Man (Today's English Version,* 1971)

Living Lessons of Life and Love (containing Ruth, Esther, Job, Ecclesiastes, and the Song of Solomon, from *The Living Bible,* 1968)

You have now used up approximately two-and-a-half inches of your one-foot shelf. So, add a Bible dictionary to help you understand better some of the very important words (not only in the Book of Job, but in the rest of the Bible). Choose one of several here (again, we list them alphabetically):

Harper's Bible Dictionary
New Westminster Dictionary of the Bible
Zondervan Pictorial Bible Dictionary

Then get a concordance. (Abridged ones always seem to lack the word for which you're looking!) This will enable you to locate all occurrences of practically all of the Bible words. Here, since the Revised Standard Concordance is quite expensive (but most useful), why not use the comparatively inexpensive *Cruden's Complete Concordance of the Old and New Testaments* (based on the *King James Version;* but you can work through this to the other translations)?

Now for a commentary. An excellent one for lay people is volume 8 of *The Layman's Bible Commentary,* which is a twenty-five-volume set of little books which may be bought separately. This is inexpensive and extremely helpful. The volume covers Ezra, Nehemiah, Esther, and Job. Another commentary which you might like to include is Hanson and Hanson's book entitled *Job.* Or some may prefer to purchase a one-volume commentary on the whole Bible, such as the new *Interpreter's One-Volume Commentary on the Bible.*

For other helps, let's mention only two more types. Many have found the "study Bible" to be very handy, most useful. The brief introductions to the Biblical books plus the selective footnotes in the *Oxford Annotated Bible* (RSV text) have proved themselves invaluable to many students. *Harper's Study Bible* is also used widely.

Two much more general but extremely helpful works (both in paperback editions) are:

Alan Richardson's *A Theological Word Book of the Bible*
Leslie Weatherhead's *Why Do Men Suffer?*

These will fill up the last of the twelve inches of space. The only thing left to do after getting the books is to make good use of them!